T0270672

Personality and Worldview

Personality and Worldview

J. H. Bavinck

TRANSLATED AND EDITED BY

James Eglinton

Foreword by Timothy Keller

WHEATON, ILLINOIS

Library of Congress Cataloging-in-Publication Data

Names: Bavinck, J. H. (Johan Herman), 1895–1964, author. | Eglinton, James Perman, translator, editor. | Keller, Timothy, 1950– writer of foreword.
Title: Personality and worldview / J. H. Bavinck ; translated and edited by James Eglinton ; foreword by Timothy Keller.
Other titles: Persoonlijkheid en wereldbeschouwing. English
Description: Wheaton, Illinois : Crossway, [2023] | Originally published in Dutch as Persoonlijkheid en wereldbeschouwing by J. H. Kok in 1928. | Includes bibliographical references and index.
Identifiers: LCCN 2022025603 (print) | LCCN 2022025604 (ebook) | ISBN 9781433584831 (hardcover) | ISBN 9781433584848 (pdf) | ISBN 9781433584862 (epub)
Subjects: LCSH: Personality. | Soul. | Spiritual life.
Classification: LCC BF698 .B31925 2023 (print) | LCC BF698 (ebook) | DDC 155.2—dc23/eng/20221017
LC record available at https://lccn.loc.gov/2022025603
LC ebook record available at https://lccn.loc.gov/2022025604

Crossway is a publishing ministry of Good News Publishers.

VP			32	31	30	29	28	27	26	25	24	23
15	14	13	12	11	10	9	8	7	6	5	4	3	2	1

To the memory of my late and dear friend
Dr. Javier Alejandro Garcia (1987–2021),
a Christian theologian who excelled in personality and worldview.

Contents

Foreword

I COULD NOT BE HAPPIER that Johan Herman Bavinck's *Personality and Worldview* has been made accessible to the English-speaking world. It is an important work, perhaps even what we call a "game changer."

The idea that Christian beliefs constitute a unique worldview—through which we view all reality and because of which we work distinctly in every area of life—has been influential in the United States for at least a century, as James Eglinton notes in his introductory essay. But the concept of worldview has lost its luster for many in the US church. I've spoken to numerous young Christians who want to lay it aside. Why? Because they say it is

- *too rationalistic*: It casts Christianity as a set of propositions or bullet points conveyed by argument in a classroom. The emphasis on worldview can give the impression that the work of the kingdom of God is mainly an intellectual or scholarly project. The role of imagination and story on worldview—or their function even *as* worldview—is simply not considered.
- *too simplistic*: The emphasis on the coherence of worldviews ("that these beliefs always lead to these outcomes") does not account for the reality that people are happily inconsistent and seem to live out of a patchwork of somewhat incoherent beliefs and worldviews.
- *too individualistic*: "Worldview thinking," at least as it exists now, seems to ignore the profound role of community and

culture on us. It implies that we are primarily the product of our individual thinking and choices. In this the current concept of worldview may be more American than biblical. We don't see that worldview is the product of communal formation and of the common stories that our community uses to make sense of life.

- *too triumphalist*: The emphasis on the antithesis of believing and unbelieving starting points, of foundational beliefs or presuppositions, can lead to a sense that we have all the truth and no one else has any at all. And in its worst usage, all sorts of contestable cultural and political opinions can be claimed to be simply part of *the* "biblical worldview" and therefore beyond questioning.

J. H. Bavinck's *Personality and Worldview* addresses these concerns and provides a far more nuanced understanding of worldview that, in my opinion, largely escapes these critiques.

His emphasis on worldview's relationship to personality shows that worldview is much more than a set of bullet points on a blackboard. This approach guards against seeing worldview as a mere intellectual framework passed on by intellectual means. *Personality and Worldview* casts worldview as not only something that forms but also something we deploy in becoming more thoughtful and "objective" in our formation.

His unique contribution—the distinction between a "worldvision" and a "worldview"—explains why so few people live out of a consistent and coherent worldview. The worldvision (or world "mindset" or "mentality") is a set of basic intuitions picked up from our environment, consisting in simplistic and reductionistic ideas through which we view reality as through spectacles. A worldview, however, is more like a map, never fully finished in this life, in which we work out the implications of Christianity for every area of life in our time and place.

Bavinck's emphasis on psychology entails community formation (though he often leaves that implicit). *Personality and Worldview* in many ways reflects the psychology of an earlier time, and yet it recognizes that our "personality" is not only, as Eglinton explains, the result of "the idiosyncrasies of [our inborn] temperament[s]" but "a set of intuitions about the world formed in all individuals by their family and home environment, their teachers and education, and the broad culture within which they live."[1] Here *Personality and Worldview* anticipates Charles Taylor's concept of worldview as a "social imaginary"—the way a community of people learn to imagine the world.[2]

Finally, the Bavincks' emphasis on worldview as what James Eglinton, Gray Sutanto, and Cory Brock have previously described as mapmaking is a crucial idea.[3] Developing a worldview is an effort to transcend the limitations and reductionisms of our worldvision. If a worldview is something we painstakingly work out our whole lives, several things follow:

1. Worldview is not in this metaphor a finished weapon to be wielded against opponents—it guards against triumphalism in that regard.
2. It's always somewhat unfinished and growing. That is humbling as well.
3. A Christian in Indonesia would not be developing the exact same map as a Christian in Scotland. If you are applying the Christian's doctrines to all of life, the questions and issues one faces will differ in different places. As such, although *Personality and Worldview* doesn't say this explicitly, it gives us the basis for the thought that there may be overlapping and noncontradictory but somewhat different Christian worldviews in different cultures. That also undermines triumphalism.

---

1 See p. 12.
2 See Charles Taylor, *Modern Social Imaginaries* (Durham, NC: Duke University Press, 2004); Taylor, *A Secular Age* (Cambridge, MA: Belknap Press of Harvard University Press, 2007).
3 Nathaniel Gray Sutanto, James Eglinton, and Cory C. Brock, "Editors' Introduction," in Herman Bavinck, *Christian Worldview* (Wheaton, IL: Crossway, 2019), 16–17.

For these reasons and more, I am so grateful for James Eglinton's translation of *Personality and Worldview* and his introduction. Read them both carefully, and think out the implications for how you are understanding and practicing your faith in the world today.

TIMOTHY KELLER
New York City
May 2022

Acknowledgments

I AM GRATEFUL to a number of people whose kindness made this book possible, not least several members of the Bavinck family itself. Professor Maarten Bavinck, a grandson of J. H. Bavinck, graciously granted permission for the work to be translated into English. My own first exposure to *Personality and Worldview* came about in 2010, when Wim Bavinck and Emelie Bavinck–van Halsema gifted me several boxes of books by their illustrious relatives. It was a joy to discover J. H. Bavinck's lost treasure in the midst of those works. To each of you, *van harte bedankt*. I hope you are pleased with the English version of this book.

Once again, it has been a pleasure to produce a book with Crossway. I owe a debt of gratitude, in particular, to Justin Taylor and David Barshinger, whose enthusiasm, professionalism, vision, and patience have played no small part in keeping this project moving along toward completion.

I am also thankful to a group of fine PhD students—Hunter Nicholson, Terence Chu, Israel Guerrero, Chun Tse, Ray Burbank, Henry Chiong, Sebastian Bjernegård, David Meinberg, and Nathan Dever—and to my colleague Ximian (Simeon) Xu, who gathered week by week at the University of Edinburgh to read through the chapters together. My friends (and former PhD students) Gray Sutanto, Cory Brock, and Greg Parker each read the manuscript and provided valuable feedback. As ever, Marinus de Jong patiently answered queries about grammatical complexities and fine shades of meaning in the original text. Thanks to you all.

Finally, I owe a special word of appreciation to Tim Keller, a friend and mentor who provided the foreword and has been a source of constant encouragement at each stage of translation and production.

Editor's Introduction

PERSONALITY AND WORLDVIEW. In the early twenty-first-century West, those words summon a range of ideas—some bland, others deeply controversial.

Personality: Context and Knowledge

To many, the language of *personality* is used to talk about an individual's capacity for extroversion and fun. In that manner of speaking, a particularly dull person might be seen as having no personality at all, whereas a very outgoing person is assumed to have personality in abundance. In that sense, it is a superficial term.

Increasingly, though, *personality* is used with more depth by a generation that relies on Myers-Briggs tests and the Enneagram to decode the reality that we all have a personality of one sort or another. To this more savvy (mostly millennial) crowd, personality involves introversion as much as extroversion. Their more nuanced approach assumes that every personality is ordered in a particular way—and that the makeup of your personality is both innate and unchangeable. As such, the result of a personality test functions as a kind of self-revelation: it purports to tell you who you really are, what you are truly like, so that a newfound self-knowledge will somehow reconcile you to yourself. Pay enough attention to your preset personality type, we are told, and you can more intentionally build your life around it.

That view is unsettling to some and is certainly met with skepticism by many: How do I know the test is reliable? And what if I dislike the personality type it reveals?

Worldview: Contested and Neglected

Depending on where you are in the world, the term *worldview* is different. In North America, embattled and riven as it is by culture wars, *worldview* is a hotly contested term. For some in this setting, the notion of worldview functions as a source of stability. As a concept, it represents a grouping of basic, deeply held commitments that shape both a culture and the lives of those who inhabit it. Everyone has a worldview, the idea goes, for which reason it is important that you know which worldview you adhere to and whether yours is the right one.

As with the millennials whose personality tests serve to reveal who they truly are as individuals, worldview can also function as a source of self-revelation, albeit the revelation of who your group really is and what it is truly like. (And conversely, it reveals who the other groups are and what they are really like: those who have secular, humanist, Islamic, Buddhist, and so on, worldviews.)

In the context of culture-war America, the idea of a biblical worldview has a particular hold on the American evangelical imagination: there is no shortage of online "biblical worldview tests" that will quickly reveal the makeup of your own worldview and judge whether it is adequately biblical or of polls that assert a connection between worldview and lifestyle. In that culture, part of the allure of a biblical worldview is the apparent ease with which it can be attained. It lends itself well to a list of points on a whiteboard and to online videos that promise to equip the viewer with a biblical worldview in a matter of minutes. Assent to the key propositions presented, and you can confidently state that you "have a biblical worldview."

In North America, of course, the notion of worldview also draws fierce criticism. Some see it as simplistic, reductive, and blinkered, arguing that its apparent transparency (in its emphasis on beliefs clearly projected outward) is an illusion. In that line of critique, worldview is perceived as something of a Trojan horse—a word that distracts the listener from hidden assumptions that serve the interests of the powerful white evangelical men who support worldview-based thinking. Critics of worldview commonly assert that the idea was invented by Immanuel Kant (1724–1804)—who coined the German equivalent, *Weltanschauung*—and has no prior history to that, a claim flatly contradicted by supporters of worldview who acknowledge that while the label is a relative newcomer on the historical scene, its substance has a much longer lineage. In *Worldview: The History of a Concept*, for example, David Naugle describes a theologized way of interpreting life and the world as far predating Kant's intervention, citing early-church figures such as Augustine (354–430) alongside medieval and early modern theologians such as Thomas Aquinas (1225–1274), Martin Luther (1483–1546), and John Calvin (1509–1564) as older examples of those whose commitment to worldview-based thinking was identifiable in all but name.[1]

Meanwhile, in the United Kingdom, *worldview* is a largely unknown term that draws little to no reaction from most. In a culture profoundly shaped by the heritage of Anglophone philosophy, talk of worldview is far more likely to draw blank stares than heated debate. British culture is a distinct cocktail of common-sense epistemology and empiricism, and it rests on the belief that human beings are (or, if they learn to think properly, can become) epistemologically neutral, unbiased, and presuppositionless in their judgments. As such, the story goes, they are able to think with unclouded judgment about self-evident truths. As those who believe that their take on the world is both correct and obvious, most Brits feel no need for a worldview concept. Indeed, worldview is a strikingly un-British idea. It undermines the very notion of Britishness, recasting it as a kind of cognitive dissonance, a suspension of disbelief in the reality that all human life is grounded on *a priori* starting points that are often utterly arbitrary, unempirical, and in no

---

1   David K. Naugle, *Worldview: The History of a Concept* (Grand Rapids, MI: Eerdmans, 2002), 5.

way common or sensical to all peoples. The language of *worldview* did not grow naturally in British cultural soil, tilled for so long, as it has been, by the philosophies of John Locke (1632–1704) and David Hume (1711–1776). Empires are not founded on admissions of arbitrariness or terms that point beyond themselves in the way that *worldview* gestures toward the heft of other worldviews. By necessity, an empire needs to be the only show in town.

None of this is to say, of course, that British culture has no need of a worldview concept. In the early twenty-first century, and due in large part to the history of immigration facilitated by Britain's colonial past, the United Kingdom is increasingly diverse in terms of culture, epistemology, religion, and ethnicity. Sustained immigration from the non-Western world has challenged typically British claims to neutrality, common sense, and obviousness. Seemingly universal ideas like *neutral* and *common* now look awkwardly parochial and untenable. To some, *these* are the words that distract the listener from hidden assumptions that serve the interests of those who claim to look on the world without bias or presuppositions.

Despite this cultural background, one segment of British society continues to cling tightly and loudly to the tenets of Anglophone philosophy: the secular humanists. Elevating the natural sciences into a form of scientism, secular humanism deals exclusively in the currency of non-subjective thinking, universally self-evident truths, and claims to the obviousness of an antireligious life. As a movement, it is as British as can be. Faced with this philosophy, British Christianity—in some quarters, at least—has begun to turn to the language of *worldview* in an attempt to articulate the sense in which secular humanism is not self-evident to those who are not secular humanists. The British church's efforts, however, are tentative. *Worldview* may be easier to pronounce than *Weltanschauung*, but in saying it, Brits are still learning to speak a foreign tongue.

The Americanization of a Dutch Idea

In comparison to this, it is all the more interesting that a large section of American Christianity speaks the language of *worldview* with ease.

I describe this as noteworthy because, for the most part, American culture rests on the same bedrock of Anglophone philosophy. In complex ways, American evangelicalism is also influenced by the same philosophical tendencies. Why have British and American cultures been so different in their receptivity to *worldview*?

In the melting pot that is American culture, worldview-based thinking arrived through the sustained immigration of Dutch Reformed Christians to North America. Their Old World (Continental) philosophical heritage was shaped by a distinct breed of philosophers: the likes of René Descartes (1596–1650) and Baruch Spinoza (1632–1677), who eschewed supposedly neutral starting points and instead spoke of presuppositions as universal but also as arbitrary and varied. From Spinoza, the Dutch imagination had learned to appreciate that all human thinking begins with untested assumptions. From Descartes, the Dutch mind learned to subject even those assumptions to critical scrutiny. On the path to his famous dictum "I think, therefore I am," Descartes argued that everything—even the *a priori* presuppositions that steer our most basic intuitions—can and must be subject to radical doubt.

Alongside this philosophical heritage, Dutch Reformed immigrants brought with them a habit of instruction in the theology of the Heidelberg Catechism. That catechism's epistemology is far removed from the commonsense, evidentialist, empiricist philosophy (and theology) that emerged in the English-speaking world. Rather than addressing its readers on the basis of unaided human reason, it begins (as similar catechisms by Luther and Calvin do) with an exposition of the Apostles' Creed. The Heidelberg Catechism inducts its readers into an idiosyncratic message ("the holy gospel"), which is the source of knowledge of the Christian faith as summarized in the creed, which is itself confessed by an idiosyncratic community: the church of Christ.

The Heidelberg Catechism assumes that all knowledge—Christian and non-Christian—is based in faith and thus that Christianity provides a distinct view of life and the world that proceeds from this faith. As *worldview* implicitly nods in the direction of *worldviews*, the Heidelberg Catechism's induction into the Christian faith acknowledges that human beings can also pursue a different view of life and the world that is not informed by the gospel. The Heidelberg Catechism treats Christianity as true but not as *obviously* true to all people. That distinction is both subtle and inestimably important to the kind of theology that developed in the Netherlands and that was then imported to North America.

Although the catechism does not contain the term *worldview*, its epistemology played no small part in the later growth of worldview-based thinking that would blossom in the Netherlands from the late nineteenth century onward. In that period, the Dutch Reformed church became the scene of an effort to articulate the historic Reformed faith in a way that was recognizably orthodox and modern: the neo-Calvinist movement. Led by the theologians Abraham Kuyper (1837–1920) and Herman Bavinck (1854–1921), the neo-Calvinists spoke often and explicitly of the reality and inescapability of different worldviews. They shunned the idea that the human being was a blank slate capable of neutrality or freedom from presuppositions. That kind of typically Anglophone view, they thought, was hopelessly naive and a culture-wide delusion of sorts. The concept that best expressed those denials of commonplace Anglophone tendencies was *worldview*.

On the one hand, to a neo-Calvinist, worldview entailed an acceptance that human life cannot be lived without a faith-based acceptance of *a priori* starting points. On the other, it also accepted that those starting assumptions were disordered by sin and thus would vary dramatically across the human population. Echoing their catechism, the neo-Calvinists believed that the truth of Christianity was powerfully compelling, without assuming this to be obviously or self-evidently so to all people. In contrast to their catechism, however, they employed the language of *worldview* to make precisely this point.

In *The Scandal of the Evangelical Mind*, Mark Noll described the relationship between Dutch Reformed immigrants and the broader culture of American evangelicalism. Like American evangelicals, the

Dutch Reformed held a high view of the authority of the Bible and were committed to the notion of active personal piety. That proximity allowed for an exchange of ideas in both directions: the immigrant Dutch Reformed faith underwent a general process of Americanization (and evangelicalization), while American evangelicalism gained a taste for the Dutch legacy of "serious academic work and experienced philosophical reasoning."[2]

That evangelical exposure to Dutch thought also included the notion of worldview. In that context, though, the neo-Calvinist concept of worldview also seems to have undergone a distinct kind of Americanization: subject to the conditions of American evangelicalism, the term remained the same, while the content changed somewhat. For example, when introducing our translation of Herman Bavinck's *Christian Worldview* (first published in Dutch in 1904 and released in English in 2019), Cory Brock, Gray Sutanto, and I described how Bavinck's early twentieth-century idea of Christian worldview was an essentially inductive thought process quite unlike much of the evangelical "biblical worldview" movement today:

> A worldview is a map, drawn over time from careful research, derived from actual knowledge of the geography, from pious religion, from the desire for truth, and is amenable to updating. After all, maps are made from research—some careful, meticulous, and true and some not. Some maps account for the details as they are presented, and some are false. But mapmaking we must do.[3]

For Bavinck, the task of making such a map was question driven: What am I? Where did I come from? How does my mind relate to the world beyond my sense of self? Do I know? If so, how can I know?

---

2 Mark A. Noll, *The Scandal of the Evangelical Mind* (Grand Rapids, MI: Eerdmans, 1994), 216.

3 Nathaniel Gray Sutanto, James Eglinton, and Cory C. Brock, "Editors' Introduction," in Herman Bavinck, *Christian Worldview*, trans. and ed. Nathaniel Gray Sutanto, James Eglinton, and Cory C. Brock (Wheaton, IL: Crossway, 2019), 16.

How should I act? What is the point of life? What is my life headed toward? As such, it is a thoroughly inductive way of thinking and living in pursuit of godly wisdom. Viewed in this way, a Christian worldview expands with time. It is open ended and has a gaze that is as wide as the world itself.

By contrast, much American evangelical worldview thinking is deductive and by nature restrictive. It is often an exercise in list writing and in agreeing to the contents of those lists, rather than a slow process of exploration and cartography. It arrives as a complete package and, as noted earlier, in some forms at least, can apparently be acquired through a five-minute YouTube video. Although the term *worldview* diffused from Dutch America into the evangelical mainstream, it was not left untouched by the process. As a result, to read early twentieth-century neo-Calvinists and twenty-first-century evangelicals on worldview can be a jarring experience—almost as though we are left to deal with *faux amis* (false friends). As Timothy Keller has noted in the foreword to this book, from a neo-Calvinist perspective, the American evangelical rendition of worldview is often overly rationalistic (in approaching the world via a series of propositions rather than as a way of imagining the world through community and story), simplistic (in drawing tight connections between beliefs and outcomes, as though people generally lived consistently with their beliefs), individualistic (in neglecting the role of community and culture in shaping us and in treating us as though we are the product of our own individual thinking), and, as a consequence of all this, triumphalist.

For that reason, when we released the first English translation of Herman Bavinck's *Christian Worldview*, our goal was to show the English-speaking world that the neo-Calvinist tradition approaches worldview quite differently from much of current-day evangelicalism. Our hope was to make a sparkling—but otherwise forgotten—text on worldview available to a larger audience. The same hope undergirds the effort to translate this book, *Personality and Worldview*, by Herman Bavinck's nephew and former student, the theologian, psychologist, and missiologist Johan Herman Bavinck.

Johan Herman Bavinck

Johan Herman (1895–1964) was the son of Herman Bavinck's brother Coenraad Bernardus ("Bernard") Bavinck (1866–1941), a Christian Reformed pastor and noted Augustine enthusiast. J. H. Bavinck studied under his uncle at the Free University of Amsterdam (1912–1918), where his circle of friends included Hendrik Kramer (1888–1965) and Herman Dooyeweerd (1894–1977)—contemporaries who would later be noted for their own respective contributions to missiology and philosophy. After his studies in Amsterdam, J. H. Bavinck moved to Germany to begin doctoral studies at the University of Erlangen (1918–1919), where he wrote a thesis on psychology and mysticism in the medieval German Dominican Henry Suso (1295–1366).

Doctorate in hand, Bavinck moved to Indonesia (1920), where he spent six years pastoring congregations attended by Dutch expatriates and Westernized locals. Returning to the Netherlands in 1926, he pastored a congregation in Heemstede for three years—publishing *Personality and Worldview*[4] in that period—before heading eastward again in 1930. This time, his work took a strikingly different shape. Rather than ministering to expatriates, he became something of a neo-Calvinist Hudson Taylor (1832–1905), first working as a missionary youth pastor before becoming a teacher of local pastors in Jogyakarta. He took on a Javanese name (Kjai Martawahana) and began to publish theological literature in the local language. In this second period, he gained the nickname "the white Javanese."[5] Eventually, in 1939, he returned to the Netherlands, where he spent the rest of his life teaching missiology at the Free University of Amsterdam and at the Theological School in Kampen.[6]

Some of J. H. Bavinck's works are relatively well known outside the Netherlands: among others, his books *An Introduction to the Science*

4 Johan Herman Bavinck, *Persoonlijkheid en wereldbeschouwing* (Kampen: J. H. Kok, 1928).
5 J. van den Berg, "The Legacy of Johan Herman Bavinck," *International Bulletin of Missionary Research* 7, no. 4 (1983): 172.
6 See Paul J. Visser, "Introduction: The Life and Thought of Johan Herman Bavinck," in *The J. H. Bavinck Reader*, ed. John Bolt, James D. Bratt, and Paul J. Visser, trans. James A. De Jong (Grand Rapids, MI: Eerdmans, 2013), 1–94.

of Missions, Between the Beginning and the End, The Church between Temple and Mosque, and *The Riddle of Life* have all been available in English for some time and have their own devoted following.[7] Among his writings, though, *Personality and Worldview* is a uniquely important text. Biographically, it stands between his two (distinct) periods in the East and functions as a bridge that connects these phases of his life and thought. As such, it shows us a careful Christian thinker learning to develop categories that would enable him to serve as a Reformed missionary among non-Western people, while also sharpening his own view of the cultural shifts that affected twentieth-century Westerners. Beyond that, it is perhaps the most useful text in positioning him in relation to his uncle. *Personality and Worldview* can be read as an effort to advance and further nuance Herman Bavinck's own contribution to the conversation on Christian worldview.

Worldview and Worldvision

If Herman Bavinck's *Christian Worldview* opened a new vista to Anglophone conversations around worldview, it was to show that the neo-Calvinist tradition construes worldview not as a rapid information dump—like Neo learning kung fu in *The Matrix*—or merely as a process of assent to a list of propositions. Rather, it showed that worldview is both something that is formative and something that is itself in a process of formation. It showed us Herman Bavinck's account of how worldview takes time. Properly speaking, of course, Bavinck presented a "world-and-life view" (*wereld- en levensbeschouwing*): an account of a lifelong pilgrimage toward wisdom about God, the world, and one's life within it. It encompasses both the truth about the world and about human life—your life and mine. That kind of thing cannot be rushed.

---

7   J. H. Bavinck, *An Introduction to the Science of Missions,* trans. David Hugh Freeman (Phillipsburg, NJ: P&R, 2012); Bavinck, *Between the Beginning and the End: A Radical Kingdom Vision,* trans. Bert Hielema (Grand Rapids, MI: Eerdmans, 2014); Bavinck, *The Church between Temple and Mosque: A Study of the Relationship between the Christian Faith and Other Religions* (Grand Rapids, MI: Eerdmans, 1981); Bavinck, *The Riddle of Life,* trans. Bert Hielema (Grand Rapids, MI: Eerdmans, 2016).

In *Personality and Worldview*, J. H. Bavinck adds to that vista considerably and in important ways. Above all, he does this through a creative effort to supply working terms and concepts to explain every human's starting point on the path that eventually leads toward a rich and mature worldview, while also offering an account of why most people are happy never to take a single step forward on that path. While cultures might be driven by grand worldviews, Bavinck argues that most individuals are not. To borrow the language of Isaiah 44:19 (NIV), "no one stops to think" about worldview, despite the pervasive influence worldviews have on whichever culture they inhabit and the haphazard glimpses of those worldviews that can be seen in people's lives. That kind of claim offers scope to nuance the worldview conversation considerably, and as such, it merits our detailed attention.

Advocates of worldview tend to emphasize its ubiquity (which is to say, in effect, "Worldview matters because everyone has one"). With that in mind, it is perhaps surprising that in *Personality and Worldview*, J. H. Bavinck makes the paradoxical claim that worldview is both everywhere ("Everyone has a worldview") *and* nowhere ("Almost no one has a worldview").

How can both these statements be true? How is it possible that while all people live on the basis of *a priori* starting points (which are generally taken to be the basic building blocks of worldview), worldviews—or at least, worldviews truly deserving of that name—are nonetheless as rare as hens' teeth? J. H. Bavinck's answer lies in a novel conceptual distinction between *worldvision* (which all humans have, by necessity) and *worldview* (which drives entire cultures, while being possessed by very few people).[8] In this book, we see that while we all begin life with

---

8 Prior to the publication of *Personality and Worldview*, the Dutch religious socialist Henri Wilhelm Philip Elise van den Bergh van Eysinga (1868–1920) used the terms *wereldbeschouwing* (worldview) and *wereldvisie* (worldvision). His work, however, does not offer an account of how the terms differ and seems to use them more or less interchangeably. See, for example, Henri Wilhelm Philip Elise van den Bergh van Eysinga, *Apologie en bevestiging: Nadere toelichting bij "Het bankroet van religie en Christendom in de moderne maatschappij"* (Zutphen: J. H. A. Wansleven & Zoon, 1899), 7, 23, 29, 53. Twelve years before *Personality and Worldview*, the term *wereldvisie* also appeared in a publication by

a *worldvision*, a proper *worldview* is a momentous achievement. Few individuals move from one to the other.

To provide the reader with a short, preparatory introduction to this distinction, a *worldvision* is a set of intuitions about the world formed in all individuals by their family and home environment, their teachers and education, and the broad culture within which they live. It is also closely bound to the idiosyncrasies of an individual person's temperament. That particular combination provides a workable (albeit limited) frame of reference with which to live from day to day. Indeed, it is possible to spend the entirety of your life only looking at life and the world through the single lens that is your *worldvision*. In the same sense, it is possible to spend an entire life navigating the streets of New York City only in a first-person perspective, never seeing a map of the city (and all that lies beyond it) or climbing a skyscraper in order to move from the limitations of your individual *vision* of each street to a more capacious *view* of the whole city. *Worldview* relates to *world-vision* in that sense. It elevates the limitations of first-person vision to the breadth of a bird's-eye view. An individual *vision within the world* is a necessary starting point, certainly, but it should not be confused with a capacious *view of the world*. Every individual has a *worldvision*, but few have a *worldview*.

In that setting, J. H. Bavinck's provocative claim is that each world-vision is, in essence, no more than a set of untested presuppositions about life imbibed within our home communities. (Viewed as such, worldvision functions as an equivalent concept to Charles Taylor's no-

---

J. R. Slotemaker de Bruïne, once again without an account of its relationship to *wereld-beschouwing*. See J. R. Slotemaker de Bruïne (1869–1941), *Dogmatiek en cultuur* (Utrecht: G. J. A. Ruys, 1916), 20. The only twentieth-century Dutch writer to use both *wereldvisie* and *wereldbeschouwing* in close textual proximity prior to J. H. Bavinck was the liberal theologian Gerhardus Hendericus van Senden (1884–1968). See, for example, G. H. van Senden, *Het vraagstuk van rechtzinnigheid en vrijzinnigheid* (Baarn: Hollandia-Drukkerij, 1912), 5, 24, 46. Like van den Bergh van Eysinga, van Senden does not deploy the terms as distinct concepts. Dutch sources that treat *wereldvisie* and *wereldbeschouwing* as conceptually distinctive only emerged in neo-Calvinist circles after the publication of *Personality and Worldview*. See, for example, N. W. van Diemen de Jel, *Niet onze wegen* (Kampen: J. H. Kok, 1932), 120.

tion of the "social imaginary"—the claim that humans "imagine" the world in an unconscious, pretheoretical way and live within it on that basis more so than on the basis of calculated, abstract reasoning.)[9] A worldvision is made up of utterly subjective working assumptions about the world and nothing more. It provides a means of functioning in the world but in no way offers the *truth* about that world.

Life is livable, to a degree, on the basis of a worldvision in the same way that life in the Matrix works for those who never ask, "What is the Matrix?" Some, however, desire to ask precisely that question. They become conscious that their working assumptions might not correspond to the truth, and as such, they want to put them to the test. In J. H. Bavinck's terms, that kind of person has begun a pilgrimage from the realm of the wholly subjective (a *worldvision*) toward the truly objective (a *worldview*), which is most profoundly a pilgrimage from the finite to the infinite, from the creature toward the Creator as the only one whose *view of the world* is exhaustive in knowledge and perfect in wisdom.

With this distinction, J. H. Bavinck tries to provide tools with which to understand Herman Bavinck's account of worldview as a slow process of mapmaking. To adapt one of J. H. Bavinck's own illustrations, a worldvision is like a map of the world that has been crumpled up into a paper ball. Although that ball now feels manageable in your hand, and while its visible parts offer you some tools for navigation (and a limited degree of truth about the world depicted), it nonetheless must be uncrumpled. The map's potential far exceeds whatever the crumpled ball can offer.

Although Herman Bavinck did not use the language of *worldvision*, his later interpreter Lolke van der Zweep (1891–1970) argued that J. H. Bavinck's worldvision-worldview distinction was nonetheless present in his uncle's thought in all but name.[10] Commenting on Herman Bavinck's

---

9   See, for example, Charles Taylor, *Modern Social Imaginaries* (Durham, NC: Duke University Press, 2004).

10 Bavinck, *Christian Worldview*, 22; Lolke van der Zweep, *De paedagogiek van Bavinck: Met een inleiding tot zijn werken* (Kampen: J. H. Kok, 1935), 196.

statement in *Christian Worldview* that the modern age lacked a "'unified' world-and-life view," van der Zweep claimed that this comment referred not to each individual lacking a coherent take on life and the world but rather to a problem that beset modernity more generally. The modern world was not able to unite what Bavinck's nephew would term the ordinary person's worldvision and the refined thinker's worldview but instead set them in opposition. Modernity cast the untutored mind and the expert intellectual as mortal enemies.[11]

Despite that insight, however, Herman Bavinck did not provide an imaginative set of terms and concepts to articulate the complex process of worldview formation that would hold together worldvision and worldview. His work presents us with a form of mapmaking, certainly, but leaves us with important questions: What exactly does the process of cartography involve? And what of those who have no wish to consult that map as they go about their lives? In what sense is a worldview ubiquitous in such cases?

These questions are answered in *Personality and Worldview*. As a complement to the earlier cartographical picture, for example, Johan Herman adds a further useful illustration: if a worldview is a map, a worldvision is a compass. Those who have no wish to make a map, who reject the struggle to cultivate a worldview in order to remain grounded in whatever worldvision life happens to have given them, have something far more basic—a tool that orients and directs them, albeit without offering any grand *view* of the world in which they move. In that regard, the worldvision-worldview distinction is useful in building on Herman Bavinck's earlier contributions. (The careful reader will also notice that Johan Herman also pairs Herman's concepts of a world-and-life view with the terms *worldvision* and *lifevision*. Just as a world-and-life *view* deals with a true, objective knowledge of the world *and* human life, a world-and-life *vision* deals with an assumption-based, subjective knowledge of the world *and* one's own *life* in it.)

---

11   James Eglinton, "Populism vs. Progressivism: Who Knows Best?" *Christianity Today*, November 20, 2018, https://www.christianitytoday.com/.

In *Personality and Worldview*, Johan Herman also addresses his uncle's criticism of the modern tendency to set worldvision and worldview in a posture of mutual antipathy—where the sophisticated thinker looks down on the ordinary person and his rudimentary worldvision as though the intellectual person had never relied on any such thing, and where the "ordinary" person views his intellectually sophisticated neighbor with all manner of bad faith assumptions because of her education. In *Personality and Worldview*, neither worldview nor worldvision is inherently bad. In fact, quite the opposite is true. A person's worldvision is a necessary starting point in life, a location in God's good creation, a set of home coordinates somewhere in nature and history. As such, we must all begin with a worldvision and should see it as a basic good. It is by God's kind providence that no one starts off nowhere. Alongside this reality, the pursuit of a worldview *is* a noble thing. Quite strikingly, J. H. Bavinck praises this exercise of virtue in the lives of thinkers—fellow mapmakers—as diverse as Kant, Confucius (551–479 BC), and Lao-tzu (fl. 6th c. BC).

Despite this, worldvision nonetheless becomes problematic when it is made a permanent abode rather than a starting point. A worldvision shows you one way to live in the world on the basis of all manner of untested assumptions, and as such, it is utterly subjective. It is an assumption—but not the truth—about the world. It is life lived on autopilot by a passenger who as yet sits passively and unquestioningly. When a person remains in this state forever, worldvision changes from good and limited to life limiting. That person's unwillingness to ask, "What if my assumptions aren't true?" is, in effect, a self-imposed house arrest. His home coordinates become his prison because he lives without hunger for *the* truth about life, the world, and God. In light of that position, *Personality and Worldview* equips readers to think in deeply appreciative but also profoundly critical ways about worldvision. It offers a creative and somewhat experimental attempt to improve the conversation around worldview.

In what sense is the notion of worldvision experimental within this book? Although it is introduced as a prominent new concept early on, *worldvision* more or less fades into the background as the book proceeds. Once the reader has been given a clear sense of what the author means by his awkward neologism, he substitutes it with "mentality," a conventional term that has now been loaded with new meaning. Rhetorically, then, J. H. Bavinck prioritized the thinking that undergirds the idea of worldvision far more than he cared for the cumbersome label itself—a fact that might provide comfort to those who wish to explain his ideas in, say, Spanish or Portuguese, whose established terms for *worldview* (*cosmovision* and *cosmovisão*, respectively) already look and sound uncomfortably like *worldvision*.[12] Despite these limitations, J. H. Bavinck's worldvision concept remains a valuable one. It explains why so few people live out a comprehensive, consistent, and coherent worldview, while also reminding us that each person's worldvision is complex and highly individuated. Although it attunes us to the simplistic, inadequate, and reductionistic slogans that many people live by, the worldvision notion itself helps us guard against simplistic takes on the people who parrot them.

An Augustinian Critique of Worldview

Personality and Worldview also equips its reader to think of the notion of worldview with the same blend of appreciative critique. J. H. Bavinck was profoundly influenced by the theology and psychology of the African church father Augustine of Hippo. Indeed, it would not be an overstatement to describe the broad shape of his work (in missiology and psychology) as a modern exploration of the paradox laid out in Augustine's *Confessions*: that every human life is spent simultaneously

---

12 This may well explain why *worldvision* does not seem to become a long-standing part of J. H. Bavinck's vocabulary in subsequent writings. After *Personality and Worldview*, it is used sparingly indeed. In a rare example in 1932, we find him using the term as a corrective to a speaker who used "life feeling" (*levensgevoel*) and "worldview" as synonyms. "Dr. B.," we read, "would actually rather swap the term worldview for worldvision." See J. H. Bavinck, "De Christelijke grondslagen van ons onderwijs," in *Tweede christelijk onderwijs congres te houden op 11 en 12 april 1939 te Bandoeng* (Bandoeng: Visser, 1932), 212. The original Dutch reads, *Levensgevoel en wereldbeschouwing. Dr. B. zou hier eigenlijk het woord wereldbeschouwing willen vervangen voor wereldvisie.*

running toward *and* away from God. That psychological paradox plays a central role in J. H. Bavinck's understanding of worldview building, which he understood to be a very human attempt to move toward *and* evade God. In the same paragraph, for example, he writes that "all seeking for a worldview is, in the deepest sense, always a seeking after God" and that "every worldview . . . is a fleeing from God, a pulling back from God, a not daring to accept God."[13]

That kind of Augustinian reminder about human worldviews is a humbling one, and it bespeaks Johan Herman's own capacity for profound psychological insight. It also provides the backdrop to his account of the Christian gospel as a worldview unto itself, as something that rebuilds each uniquely disordered human being from the ground (which is to say, worldvision) up. As a worldview, the gospel remolds but does not destroy individual personality. By setting both concepts—personality and worldview—in relationship to the gospel itself, J. H. Bavinck aimed to show that worldview is much more than a list of bullet points to which one must assent. Rather, it is almost a synonym for sanctification. It lays hold on us, and we press on toward it. Worldview has a formative power over us, while also being something we deploy in learning to become more thoughtful and closer to the objective truth, as we live *coram Deo* in the world.

Theology for Life in the World

Thus far, this introduction has said far more about worldview (and worldvision) than personality. Why did J. H. Bavinck write a book that attempted to deal with both? The contents of this book first saw the light of day as public lectures given to engineering students at the Delft University of Technology in the winter of 1927. Its original audience, then, was not made up of pastors or theologians. In fact, the clarity and originality of the talks meant that as his series progressed, the regular audience grew beyond the student community. He gradually found himself speaking to a broad and general public—which soon began

13 See pp. 38, 39.

asking for the lectures to be published in book form (and they were the following year).

In those lectures, he primarily addressed a group of young Reformed Christians who had grown up in a culture dominated by neo-Calvinistic worldview thinking and within which Abraham Kuyper's own example had created a widespread tendency to reduce people (and their personalities) to whatever worldview they supported. In their youthful eyes, worldview seemed to quash the very thing that their lived, modern experience pointed toward: individuality. Although Bavinck's lectures were given decades before the outbreak of the revolutionary individualism of the 1960s, he was addressing precisely that mid-twentieth century context, albeit at an earlier developmental stage. The same sort of antiworldview critiques now heard in American evangelicalism were heard in the Netherlands in the 1920s: worldviews are facades, illusions, Trojan horses that subjugate us to the personality types of the men whose names they bear, whereas human life is spontaneous, free, and unbound by abstract worldview claims. To be sure, these critiques are neither unimportant nor foolish. As humans, we experience agency. We do not seem to be machines, despite the reality of our place in a cosmos that operates on the basis of cause and effect. Why shouldn't personality trump worldview?

In response to these criticisms, J. H. Bavinck believed that a livable philosophy must strive to hold to that particular paradox—the twin poles of freedom and boundness, of acting and being acted on—rather than invest everything on one side. His response to "personality *versus* worldview" was to write *Personality and Worldview*. Of course, he was certainly not the first thinker to demonstrate such harmonizing instincts. We might think of Kant's denial of the skeptical philosopher Hume's insistence that humans are only material beings in a material world. In response, Kant argued that human life is properly livable only if we see ourselves as subject to the laws of cause and effect *phenomenally*, while having free and active agency *noumenally*. Later, the theologian Friedrich Schleiermacher (1768–1834) argued that human consciousness senses itself to be both free and dependent within the world. To insist on only one of these, he thought, was to do a grave injustice to our humanity. J. H. Bavinck follows in their nonreductionist line: to pit personality *against* worldview and insist that we must choose one or the other is no more tenable than the choice to affirm either our sense of free will or our sense of being bound. Both must be true, hence a book on personality *and* worldview.

That observation takes us to the book's closing argument, where the relationship of personality to worldview—and in particular, the place of each individual personality between the poles of worldvision and worldview—reaches a crescendo. Like an early twentieth-century Tom Holland,[14] J. H. Bavinck argues that the Christian worldview is far more important than individualistic late-modern Westerners usually realize. Although very few individuals master and embody a worldview, worldviews nonetheless master and animate entire cultures and civilizations. In that light, Bavinck portrays the late-modern secular West as unwittingly living off borrowed Christian capital in order to prop up new world-and-life views that, thus far at least, have only ever run at a deficit. While every individual is unique, there is a distinct kind of modern Western personality that takes shape through Western culture's love-hate relationship to Christianity. As Bavinck states,

> Worldviews last for longer than one generation. One generation can celebrate worldviews that provide no foundation for its own life and without that generation's exterior taking on noticeable damage. This is so because for all of us, our hearts are unconsciously so Christian.[15]

The book ends, though, with an alarming call. Eventually, J. H. Bavinck forecast, this borrowed capital will dry up, and Western culture will become something new: a culture that "has no life-nourishing and life-directing idea and therefore also no unity in living and thinking."[16] The "culture of death" that has marked the West from World War II

14 Tom Holland, *Dominion: The Making of the Western Mind* (London: Little, Brown, 2019).
15 See p. 177.
16 See p. 177.

onward, so ably described by the Jewish sociologist Philip Rieff (1922–2006), illustrates that warning.[17] In that regard, these lectures to engineering students have an edge that is almost prophetic.

Although the book is eerily ahead of its time in that regard, it also reads as dated in some respects. For example, the view of medieval monasticism advanced by J. H. Bavinck—that someone entered the monastery as a way of withdrawing from the study of nature—has now been thoroughly debunked by Seb Falk's outstanding *The Light Ages*.[18] Similarly, while Bavinck's account of the Renaissance as the birth of radical individualism (and a freedom from the tyranny of all prior sources of authority) had some support in his day,[19] contemporary readers will more likely see the Renaissance as a rediscovery of ancient (and non-Christian) sources. The book's handling of East and West will displease some readers, who will certainly find his brushstrokes uncomfortably broad—as, perhaps, they will also find uncomfortable his tendency to view the diversity of Eastern religions and cultures through what appears to be a primarily Buddhist lens.

Clearly, it is not a perfect book. Nonetheless, it received critical acclaim in its own day, even beyond the boundaries of Bavinck's own neo-Calvinist circles.[20] Although it featured regularly in Dutch discussions on worldview in the 1930s, those references began to peter out in the 1940s, after which it became a forgotten text. Opened afresh nine decades later, the book has aged remarkably well. Despite its imperfections, it speaks into our age's debates on personality and worldview—

---

17 Philip Rieff, *Sacred Order / Social Order*, vol. 1, *My Life among the Deathworks: Illustrations of the Aesthetics of Authority* (Charlottesville: University of Virginia Press, 2006).

18 Seb Falk, *The Light Ages: A Medieval Journey of Discovery* (London: Penguin, 2021).

19 Although J. H. Bavinck does not name the sources that shape his account of the Renaissance, he appears to hold to Jacob Burckhardt's (1818–1897) view that the Italian Renaissance birthed the modern individual. See Burckhardt, *The Civilization of the Renaissance in Italy* (London: Penguin, 1990).

20 In one memorable review, published in the theologically liberal newspaper *De blijde wereld*, the avowedly "not orthodox" reviewer praised J. H. Bavinck's writing as "orthodoxy at its best," before concluding, "I hope very much that this book will be read in our circles." See W. B., "Belangrijks uit boek en tijdschrift," *De blijde wereld: Christen-socialistisch weekblad*, May 11, 1929.

addressing both those who think very highly of worldview and those who give it no glory at all—with a voice that is fresh and imaginative in equal measure. For that reason, and with the kind permission of Professor Maarten Bavinck, Johan Herman's grandson, now, at long last, it has been exhumed, dusted off, and given a new lease on life in the English language.

Note on the Text

J. H. Bavinck was a master of clear, crisp, vividly illustrative Dutch prose. If anything, his skill in writing makes his work all the more challenging to translate, particularly if something of the liveliness of the original is to be carried over into a new language. For that reason, I have tried to balance, on the one hand, close equivalence of idiom and word choice between the Dutch original and its English rendering and, on the other hand, the need for the translation to flow smoothly for native English readers. The end result is, I hope, faithful to the Dutch but free from the subtle and unwieldy influence of Dutchisms. To achieve that aim, it has sometimes been necessary to clarify the meaning of Bavinck's sentences by adding illuminative words. These are always indicated to the reader in brackets.

The original text contains terms and quotations in German, Latin, and French, which needed no translation for the original audience. These have been retained (with foreign-language terms in brackets in the main text and foreign-language quotations moving into the footnotes) and translated in this edition. Where awareness of specific Dutch terms used by Bavinck might help some to read the text with greater nuance, I have retained the original Dutch in brackets.

In following the conventions of his day, Bavinck often referred to other works without providing references and mentioned many figures who were well known to his audience (playwrights, artists, scholars, historical figures, and so on) but who might be less universally recognized today. I have provided references to these works in the footnotes, as well as short historical introductions to the individuals named. These explanatory footnotes are clearly indicated as my own additions to the text. Also, Bavinck included dates for figures in only a handful of instances; for consistency, I have moved those dates to the editorial footnotes, where I have also supplemented my historical introductions with other individuals' dates.

Beyond that, as a custodian of this text, I have tried to handle it with a light touch, leaving as few of my own fingerprints on Bavinck's work as possible and making my own presence as its translator and editor otherwise inconspicuous.

JAMES EGLINTON
Edinburgh
May 2022

1

The Struggle for a Worldview

THE SUBJECT THAT WE WILL DISCUSS is beautiful and dangerous in equal measure: beautiful because it compels us to see [all] the
worldviews that have been devised as expressions of personalities, as
revelations of the soul, and dangerous because it could also cause us
to lose our own firm foundations.

Before we move forward, it is necessary, first, that we consider the
question [of personality and worldview] clearly and that we take account of the difficulties that will be placed before us. We should not
walk into the labyrinth of opinions blindly. Rather, we must reflect
beforehand on the problems that will be posed to us. If we fail to do
this, we will be in great danger of losing our way.

The history of human thought presents us with a range of ideas, of
systems, of worldviews. Some are elegant and religious, others crude
and banal. Some are deep and beautiful, others hard and ugly. Some
expand your view, lift you up, satisfy the heart, and make life appear
different; others are like sticks of dynamite that possess the power to
damage and destroy everything in their path. Some are poetic, intuitive,
thoughtful; others are based on a mass of arguments, crawling forward,
as it were, from one conclusion to another. Each of these worldviews
has enjoyed a period of recognition. When each was first proposed,
there was a group that received and honored its thoughts. But as the
years came and went, the movement [generated by it] and faith [in it]

waned, and other thinkers arose to open up new perspectives. And so human thought developed, sliding from worldview to worldview. Each system of thought must always give way to another.

The question has been posed, Must we accept that a certain development can be perceived in all those worldviews? Is there an approach to the truth [in them]? Are we moving further [forward], step by step? Are the questions posed in a more refined way, the challenges better gauged, the puzzles better solved? In one way or another, that great competition of thought must have an end point, a goal. Can we say that the history of philosophy, of worldviews in general, is the history of the discovery of the truth? Or must we think of it in a completely different way? Must we declare that the truth has never been found, that we tumble from one confusion to the next, that no progress can be observed?

This question becomes more difficult when we notice that the number of worldviews is relatively small and that the same types [of worldviews] return again and again. Kant[1] has said that the great questions regarding worldview are always these three: What can I know [*weten*]?[2] What must I do? What may I hope? Now in broad terms, only a few answers are possible to each of these questions. What can I know [*weten*]? Can I indeed know something (skepticism)? Does my knowledge [*kennis*][3] reach nothing beyond the phenomena, the externals (positivism)? Or can I proceed to the essential, the eternal, the idea, the very highest reason? In my knowing [*weten*], am I dependent, above all, on experience, sensation, perception (empiricism)? Or is it precisely the

---

1   Immanuel Kant (1724–1804), a Prussian philosopher whose work was central to the Enlightenment.—Ed.

2   Dutch uses two distinct verbs, *kennen* and *weten*, for "to know." *Kennen* refers to immediate, personal knowledge, whereas *weten* refers to more objective, reflective knowledge. In English, this corresponds to the difference between an impersonal knowledge (*weten*) of facts about someone (for example, "I know that he has red hair") and a personal knowledge (*kennen*) of that person (for example, "I know him"). Because these verbs deal with conceptually distinct forms of knowledge, where relevant I have indicated in brackets which verb the original text uses.—Ed.

3   *Kennis* (knowledge) is the noun corresponding to the verb *kennen*. It refers to knowledge that is immediate and personal.—Ed.

understanding, thinking, reason that must be honored as the highest source of knowledge (rationalism)? May I accept that my consciousness, my representations, correspond to a reality beyond myself (realism)? Or must I believe that only those representations, those concepts and thoughts, exist and that there is no material reality that corresponds to them (idealism)? Does a God who brought all things into being exist? And if he exists, how and where must I conceive of him? Is he only exalted high above the world, unknowable [onkenbaar], inaccessible (deism)? Or is he only in the world, a part of the world—that is, is the world itself God (pantheism)? Or is he both simultaneously in the world and also exalted far above it, immanent and at the same time transcendent (theism)? Or is there absolutely no higher power—that is, does everything boil down to matter and power (materialism)?

In this way, we can expand the questions on every side, although only a few answers are possible to each of these questions. The number of ideas, the number of worldviews, is limited and also must be limited. Naturally, all sorts of different forms and styles of worldview can be found. The great and basic assumptions, however, must remain the same.

It is also evident that in the course of history, the same ideas and systems return time and time again. In more recent philosophy, we find the philosophical schools of antiquity returning in new garments. We continually encounter the same constructions. It seems as though history is constantly repeating itself. What we think and the solutions we see were also grasped many centuries ago. The same forms return incessantly in the rhythm of human living and thinking. Yes, and not only that: even the order is often the same. The same development that you can see in Greek philosophy, the progress of the one system to another, you find returning at a number of points in the newer philosophy. It moves along the same paths from the one to the other:

> What has been is what will be,
>> and what has been done is what will be done,
>> and there is nothing new under the sun. [Eccl. 1:9]

And yet we must be on our guard against all one-sidedness because while they often are the same systems, that does not mean that there is indeed no difference or even a certain kind of progress. On all sorts of points, the consequences are better felt, the gaps are better filled in. It is not in vain that our era possesses wonderful material from the experiences of previous generations. When the old returns, it is never entirely the same. There is always newness and freshness in it. But nonetheless, the fact that the history of human seeking always returns to older solutions is enough to make us skeptical toward the question whether we can speak of an approach to the truth.

That is also the reason that many in our time are inclined to consider the development of worldviews from a different angle. They ask the question differently and look for a different perspective. It is foolishness, they say, to expect any progress from all that thinking and seeking. We do not know [*weten*] and will never know. We act more smartly and precisely[, they say,] when we move beyond all those worldviews to the personalities that created them. Why is it that one person chooses materialism, while another despises and detests that same materialism? Why is it that that one thinker is immediately inclined to one solution, and another goes down a different path from the beginning? What phenomenon is the cause of Spinoza[4] thinking differently from Kant, of Kant seeing things differently from Hegel?[5] Is it not this, [they allege,] that Kant was a wholly different person, a wholly different personality, from Spinoza? Is each worldview not grounded in personality? As an approach to the truth, [we are told,] it is worthless. But as a revelation of the life of the personality, it is of great significance. From Kantian philosophy we get to know Kant himself; his soul is opened up before us. Each period, each century, has its own mentality and thus also its own worldview. From the history of worldviews, we become acquainted with the history of personalities. We understand the soul better; we

---

4   Baruch Spinoza (1632–1677), a Dutch philosopher of Portuguese Sephardic Jewish extraction. Spinoza is considered one of the great rationalist philosophers of the Enlightenment.—Ed.

5   Georg Wilhelm Friedrich Hegel (1770–1831), a German idealist philosopher.—Ed.

understand the idiosyncrasy of the different sorts of people who have spoken in those worldviews. That is the worth of all those systems. They do not bring us closer to the truth, but they bring us further in the knowledge of the soul, in the knowledge of personality. A materialist does not only think differently from an idealist; he also lives differently, and he is also different. Therefore, [we hear,] the arguments they use against each other are so fruitless. Each sees things from his own personality: "Whatever sort of philosophy one has is dependent on what sort of a person one is."[6]

At first glance, there is much in this idea that is attractive. Is it not true that a person's worldview is most closely connected to his personality? Is that not the reason that humanity continually returns to the same possibilities? The possibilities of the personality are, of course, always limited. Is that not also the reason that it is so difficult to resolve the striving between worldviews with arguments? An intimate connection must exist between personality and worldview; each worldview can be fully understood only from the personality that created it.

From the Christian perspective, these things are, in a certain sense, even more obvious. If the worldview one depends on is based only on a rational understanding, the only consequence would be a struggle of ideas, and then the struggle against the Christian faith would become incomprehensible. The reason the battle of worldviews is so often carried out with furious passion would not be understandable because everything would be a great and convivial discussion of proof against proof, of one theory against another hypothesis. That, however, never seems to have been the case in history. In worldviews, personalities —human souls—battle against each other. Each defends his own life, his own character. The arguments that were advanced serve his personality's right to continue existing. That is also what every person,

---

6   The original German reads, *Was für eine Philosophie man hat, hängt davon ab was für ein Mensch man ist.* This is taken from Johann Gottlieb Fichte, *Erste und Zweite Einleitung in die Wissenschaftslehre* (Hamburg: Meiner Verlag, 1961), sec. 5, 21. Fichte (1762–1814), a German idealist philosopher, goes on to describe a philosophical system as "animated by the soul" of the one who adopts it, rather than merely as "a dead appliance" that will function identically regardless of which person uses it.—Ed.

armored as such, combats and must combat in the gospel of grace that is preached in Christ Jesus. That person's personality resists [the gospel], and thus, with all the might of thinking, he must wrestle himself free of the grip of that gospel. Precisely the fact that [worldview] is about his personality and that the actual combatants—the passions of the human soul—hide themselves behind their reasonable arguments is the fact that has given the age-old war of worldviews such depth and tension.

However attractive this thought might sound, it quickly appears to be the case that great dangers also lie hidden in it. There is even something burdensome about immersing oneself in it for a moment. The great thinkers of all ages have sought and ruminated, have striven to find the truth. There is a calling for the truth, for insight, for knowledge, in the world. What would it then mean if we, who stand behind all things, at once should announce, "All that you have done has been nothing other than a reflection of what you yourself are like. You have not brought the truth any closer; you have only shown us who you are, how your personality is composed"? Should the immediate consequence that we draw not then be, "We wish never to think again. What is the benefit of all study, of immersing oneself in the great questions of life?" With contempt, the next generation will erase all your efforts, [saying,] "You have [only] laid yourself bare." All passion, all striving, all seeking would immediately be lost. We would feel like children who frolic around and play with each other, who perhaps think that what we are doing will make humanity progress, but later, in our old age, we smile back at that delusion. Is then philosophy indeed anything else than a terrible frivolity? We imagine our worldviews, dress them up in a lot of learnedness, and say that we are dealing with the truth; we try to show how things are through many objective proofs, with great calculations, and that things cannot be otherwise. Later, another generation arises and says with hilarity, "This person thinks as such because he acts as such in all his behavior, because his personality was composed as such." In one fell swoop, all my investigations, contemplations, and proofs are made worthless.

The idea that a very close connection exists between personality and worldview thus seems to bring with it, as an undeniable consequence, the idea that all our thinking and building of philosophical systems must be regarded as idle. The most complete relativism, the conviction that each thought is relative, that no truth exists that applies absolutely to all, is the logical consequence of such a probable (self-authenticating) presupposition. We never rise above the inclination, the character of our personality; we can never climb above the subjective to the objective truth. What I call truth is only true for myself; it only fits my character; I need that so-called truth, while someone else laughs at it.

A human being, however, naturally springs back from drawing this consequence. It would mean the disruption of all spiritual and moral norms. Someone who wishes to live completely free of morals would be able to say, "What do I have to do with someone else's norms and worldview? In my worldview there are no moral commands." Not only would psychology devour all philosophy, it would also devour all norms: to everyone his own standard and his own insight because there is no absolute truth and no absolute norm. Relativism is a deadly danger for each sincere and virtuous struggle for truth and right.

But alongside this, at the same time, we are given the question that we have to ask in these investigations. On the one hand, what is the connection between personality and worldview? In what sense do these two [things] belong together inseparably? And on the other hand, how must we nonetheless be on guard against the relativism that breaks up all norms? Is there an objective approaching of the truth? Does it make sense at all to think about the puzzles of existence?

We can also formulate this question differently: To what extent is each worldview the revelation of the personality that created or received it, in order that we can become acquainted with the person through that worldview? And conversely, to what extent is each worldview a more or less objective approach to the truth, so that it possesses significance and worth as such?

In these two questions, it is clear that we must guard against two answers. The first answer is, "Personality and worldview are actually one. Each worldview is nothing other than a reflection of a personality. It only bears the semblance of objectivity, but in reality it is subjective through and through." If that were true, all thinking really would be useless, and relativism in that absolute and obliterating sense would be unavoidable.

We must also be on guard against a second answer: "Personality and worldview are two utterly [different things]. You cannot come to know anything about someone's personality from his worldview. Thinking is completely detached from being. Each worldview may be seen only as an approach to the truth and must be entirely detached from the personality that created it." If that were true, the ferocity of the struggle of worldviews would be incomprehensible. In that struggle, it does seem that the personality is indeed at stake.

Thus, the truth must be enclosed between these two. It is neither the one nor the other, for which reason each worldview must be considered from a twofold viewpoint: [it is] just as much the revelation of the personality as it is an approach to the truth. These two, it seems, are intertwined, interpenetrated, and together add up to one whole.

Before we can move more deeply into this matter, we must address a few difficulties that might arise. Our subject is personality and worldview. Perhaps you might say, "Worldview? Who actually cares about worldview anymore? We are much too busy with the social survival of the fittest, and we are too engaged in all sorts of cares of a different nature to make an effort to think about a 'worldview.'"

If you should think like this, I would immediately want to say something in response: every person has a worldview, whoever he may be. Later, we will make a distinction between a worldvision and a worldview. As soon as we make that [distinction], I must modify my statement: every person has a worldvision. [At this point,] it would be best to clarify this idea through some illustrations.

Let us imagine a driver, someone whose heart's passion is racing, who functions as one with his steering wheel, and who would rather do nothing else than storm along the road at unimaginable speed. As soon as he sits at the wheel, he sees the world from a particular perspective. He has, if you will permit me this loanword, a "particular mindset" [*bepaalde instelling*]—namely, he sees everything from the viewpoint of speed. A pothole in the road, a goat, a grocer's wagon that comes around the corner, a couple of children playing, are just as much obstacles, limitations in his thirst for speed. And as such, he sees the world very simply. For him, all things are crumpled up together as obstacles. He sees them as obstacles. That the child who steps out into the road at the last moment is an only child, that he is the apple of his mother's and father's eye, remains out of view in that instant. He is a hindrance that must be avoided, that must be taken into account, but that beyond this is only experienced as an obstacle. While he is sitting behind the wheel, his "particular mindset"—which is entirely focused on the pursuit of great speeds—brings with it [the notion] that he perceives the entire world reality only as hindrance or as favor. This is then his foundation in reality, that is, what we could call his vision of things.

Now you will say, "That vision is the work of a single moment; it counts only for as long as he is driving his car." I agree with you, but we can also think about it in a more complicated, enduring way.

An officer in a war, for example, sees the enemy only from the viewpoint of combat value. That is his "mindset," which his profession, his lifework, entails. That the man before him is the father of a large family, for whom he is irreplaceable; that he is a genius, in whose death the whole world would suffer a great loss because he could bring progress to human seeking—all remains entirely outside the officer's consideration. He does not deny it, he knows well the possibility of it, but it has no significance to him. In his intuition, the great reality of the world is crumpled up in one concept: combat value. The man before him is a soldier and thus has combat value; the machine gun next to him also has combat value. The "particular mindset" in which he lives, the particular goal that he pursues, contains the [notion] that everything he encounters can be judged only on the basis of combat value. That is, to use that word again, his worldvision.

We can also think about this [concept] in ways that are firmer and less momentary.

Imagine that four people travel to a country. One is an engineer in heart and soul. He sees all that he encounters from the question "What can be made from this?" In his thoughts he imagines lines where roads could be projected, and he bores tunnels through the mountains in the places he deems best. He comes across waterfalls and in his thoughts develops a plan for how a hydroelectric station could be built there. He comes to craters and considers the ways in which sulfur mining could be attempted. In short, in all that he sees, he plays with technical ingenuity; he sees everything from that same question.

The second traveler through the same land is an economist. He studies the varieties of soil and wonders what could be grown there. In his thoughts he weighs up the possibility of acquiring laborers; he calculates eventual rentability. Everywhere he sees something with which a profit could be made. He is constantly adding up all manner of possibilities.

The third is a geologist, not only by profession but with the full love of his heart. He looks at craggy rock formations and reconstructs their history. He sees the layers of sediment carved out by mountain rivers and asks himself how those layers developed in the past. He studies the layers of earth that are clearly visible here and there, in places where landslides caused the soil to sag. He wonders about the places from which he might expect important discoveries.

And the fourth, finally, is a poet, an artist. He listens to the secret rustling of the evening in the dark and ancient forest. He sees the mountains turn blue and is enraptured by the overwhelming majesty of pristine nature.

At the end of their journey, the four happen to come together and, when they speak to one another, ask each other, "What is the world?"

The world, so says the first, is an endless source of technical possibility. In itself, it is not yet anything, but everywhere it offers opportunity for the application of human faculties. It is a wonderful combination of energy that can be mastered and utilized by the intellect.

The world, so says another, is riches, a constant source of benefits, of the possibility of life.

The world, says the geologist, is history, always renewing itself and expanding into different formations. It is a steady process of transformation.

And the poet finally decides, the world is beauty, full of contrast and yet also of harmony, rugged and yet majestically united. It is a rhythm of flowing lines and mingling colors.

You yourself can feel it: every person sees the world from a particular perspective. That is his mentality, his goal. And that mentality always contains a particular vision of the world. The full reality of the world is never captured by any individual person. Rather, for each person it is crumpled up into a distinct whole that has meaning for him. Each mentality toward life presupposes and includes a particular worldvision.

And with this I come to the last and most difficult example. Imagine the person who lives, in practical terms, without God. If I may say it as such, God is not an item in his life's budget and plays no role in it. He acts as though there is no God. His life's mentality is atheistic. Naturally, this contains a certain worldvision, although he is not aware of it. It is the great *as though* that he has based his life on.

Or think of it differently still: in practical terms, a person lives without norms. He does what he wants, and he feels and recognizes no moral standards. In the practice of his life, he might well watch out for scandal, for punishment, but in his intimate life, he lives free of it. He also feels no sorrow for the wrong that he has done. At most, he can regret that he did not do it more efficiently. Behind that attitude to life lies a worldvision: the worldvision [that functions], namely, *as though* there are no norms, as though we are not bound by moral standards. I do not say that he would also declare this so clearly and consciously, but it is nonetheless the silent presupposition of his life. His life is based on that great *as though*. Every attitude to life, each way of life, always assumes a particular way of looking at the world, a worldvision. The simplest beggar or even a child has such a worldvision that lies at the foundation of his behavior. Life cannot be understood as anything other than a resting in a particular worldvision.

In the first place, a person makes this worldvision his own in his early years. The human being drinks in the considerations held up before him by his parents and teachers; they melt away into him and help form within him that worldvision that will serve him like a compass in later years. That often happens uncritically, it is often unconscious, and the person often does not intuit that such things have formed a worldvision within him. But the influence of that worldvision is of inestimable importance on the whole of his living and acting. In the second place, a person's worldvision is most strongly influenced by his character, predisposition, orientation. It roots around in his person and connects closely to the entirety of the tendencies of his soul. In a certain sense, it is already the presupposition of his life, before the person begins to think and begins to give an account of life and the world. Perhaps he never comes to that contemplation, never brings this further than the intuitive worldvision, *as though* there is no norm, no God, no law. In that case, the intuitive vision remains his compass in the storms of life.

It is also possible, however, that the person begins to contemplate, that he begins to ask himself whether he has the right to let his life be lived on the weak foundation of the great *as though*. Then he begins to think through whether that intuitive grasp that he made is also objectively justified, whether there really is no God and no norm, whether he has a right to [carry on] living on the basis of that presupposition. Then he tries to climb up toward the objective. The vision objectivizes itself into a worldview. He only conquers such a worldview through a great work of thinking, through quiet contemplation, through giving account of reality objectively. A worldview is not just a loose, intuitive grasp. Rather, it is supported by arguments, by motives. It clothes itself in the form of reasonableness. It is supported by logical construction. That is tiring work, a work of patience and endurance. And the fruits of it are the things given to us to consider by the history of philosophy.

I am filled with respect when I think of the great series of thinkers who have worked at the task that is a worldview. Lao-tzu[7] and Confucius,[8] the thinkers of India and of Greece, Descartes[9] and Spinoza,

---

7 Lao-tzu, a semilegendary Chinese philosopher from the sixth century BC. He is regarded as the founder of Taoism.—Ed.

8 Confucius (551–479 BC), a Chinese philosopher whose teachings gave rise to Confucianism.—Ed.

9 René Descartes (1596–1650), the French philosopher, mathematician, and scientist. Much of Descartes's life was spent in the Dutch Republic.—Ed.

Kant and Hegel. In their works lies an earnest seeking for the objective, for the certainty of the truth, so that we would be able to build our lives on it. Their thinking is an attempt to approach the riches of reality without prejudice and to search through its secrets. They struggled to free themselves from all sorts of subjective prejudices in their world-visions and to tread humbly toward the truth itself. We can indeed live *as though* there is a God or no God, *as though* there are norms or no norms, but ultimately we will want to know [*weten*] whether that great *as though* that we base our lives on can withstand the test of objective judgment. That is no game; it is not a hobby. It is alarming in its inevitability because otherwise, everything, our life itself, is a leap into the abyss. A certain self-denial is found in all philosophical thinking—the self-denial of a person who feels that the worldvision that his life's practice is built on and that is connected to his nature and character could indeed be wrong. Therein lies honesty, depth, and majesty.

As such, you sense that it is not easy to be objective. It is perhaps the weightiest demand that can ever be placed on someone—to make oneself free of the intuitive vision toward which he is naturally inclined. It is only with great difficulty that someone who is materialistic in the practice of life can proceed from objective considerations to the conclusion that it is precisely the spiritual that is central and dominant because at the moment he draws this conclusion, he judges his own life. And conversely, it is only with great difficulty that the idealist who is mystically and ascetically inclined will allow himself to be convinced of the hard, sober realness of material reality. The worldvision that lies at the basis of our character retains its influence in all thinking. In all his investigations, the person whose predisposition is strongly religious will continue to see reality differently from the person whose orientation is wholly different. Those are facts that are hard to erase. Or stated differently, a worldview distances itself from a worldvision with laborious effort, just as thinking [distinguishes itself] from living [only] with great effort. Few things require more self-denial of a person than the demand to arrive at a conclusion on objective grounds, with reasonable proofs, that is diametrically opposed to the whole composition of his life. The tension between living and thinking is very difficult, and to the earnest person, it is also a very painful tension.

From that, it is also the case that two elements are found in each worldview: the intuitive element of the subjective vision and the objective [element] of the formal, reasonable consideration. The first is the grasp that a person has on reality, in which you know [*kent*] the character, the personality. Yes, the intuitive grasp is even a revelation of personality, a confession within which he lays bare the shape of his life. The latter is the attempt at conquering the self, the honest approaching of the rich reality that can be wholly different, and much greater, than we had originally, intuitively supposed. The two elements that are enclosed within each philosophical worldview are also often very difficult to untangle. They are intertwined with one another, so that their boundaries cannot easily be identified. Each philosophy flows from personality and is at the same time an effort at conquering the self, a questioning of the objective, through which the subjective must be defined.

Yes, conquering the self—that is it. Each objectively founded worldview is a conquering of the self. It judges how our lives are composed, lays bare the deep faults therein, corrects us in every step. Hidden within it lies a deep and rich power that builds up a worldview, that regenerates. A personality ascends upward with such a worldview; it offers him a firm foundation in the whole direction of his life.

A worldview is a glorious thing. It gives rest in existence. It makes us see seemingly confusing and jagged occurrences in a particularly ordered whole. It gives us farsighted perspectives in life and the world. Intuitively, we always grasp our lives wrongly; we always try to justify ourselves and always grope in a direction that carries us to our demise. A deep and rich worldview shows us this. It corrects us. I think here of one of the mighty sayings that never fail to bring those who hear them to their senses: "The truth will set you free" [John 8:32].

The truth is not a theoretical good that you keep in a chest under many locks. The truth is of practical worth in life. It lifts you above yourself by making plain to you the faults of your own life orientation. It draws a line through your behavior; it judges your most intimate proclivities. It breaks into pieces the grasp of your worldvision, through which you had revealed your own personality and within which you could have peacefully carried on stumbling forward. It shows you the objective reality and does this with compelling power so that we should form our lives according to it. The truth sets [you] free with a great inner freedom. It sets [you] free from the sapping and errant powers that hide in a personality. It is the truth that the personality grabs onto to pull itself upward.

From that, each worldview that wrestles with an earnest and honest investigation ends with this practical demand: "If these things are so, direct your life toward them." All metaphysics ends in ethics. Every worldview ends up with "Repent! In the name of the truth, reform yourself!" Christianity wants nothing less than that. When it demonstrates the truth, it declares, "Believe and repent." There is nothing strange about that. Every worldview that lays claim to thinking—and in thinking, to life—must do the same.

A person without a worldview is a person without a firm foundation, without a compass, without a vista. He may have a worldvision; he might live, for example, as though there are no norms. But such a worldvision proceeds from himself and is rooted in his nature. He cannot pull himself upward on it, and with it he always remains on the same plane. A person with a worldview, in all cases, has light, sees more widely, more broadly, more deeply. And however much deeper and more objective that worldview is, the more it gives him stability to leave this maze of subjective inclinations and climb up to the height of the life that is grounded in the truth.

If this [principle] already applies in general, it counts in a very special sense for the truth of the gospel of Jesus Christ. That gospel offers us a worldview that smashes a person's worldvision into pieces on every side, that opposes the most intimate inclinations of the person from every side, that a human being cannot think up or invent because it was thought of by God and is given to us from God. That worldview, however, bears the objective within it to the highest degree. It cuts the human being down but at the same time gives him the stability with which he can build his life on the truth. His life's resting point is laid not in his thinking but in the truth that is shown to us in Jesus. Therefore, the worldview that is offered to us in the gospel is also of a wholly different order from every other that has been thought up and found by humans.

When we summarize our results, we then come in broad lines to the following conclusion: between philosophical worldviews (here we are treating Christianity separately because, as we said, it is of a different order) and personality, there is and must be a very close connection.

This connection is always twofold.

First, it is direct insofar as each worldview thought of by humans plays along with that person's intuitive worldvision. That vision is the revelation of his nature, of his personality. It takes root in his life, in his character. From that vision, you can get to know him.

In the second place, however, the connection between personality and worldview is also inverted insofar as each worldview is precisely an attempt to be freed from that worldvision and to approach that which is objective. There is a conquering of self in every worldview. As a rule, a person's thought is better than his life. It is by our thinking that we pull ourselves upward.

When you see these two pulling closer, you can express it in yet another way: each worldview is always two things at once, a moving toward the truth and a fleeing from the truth. It is an approaching of the truth insofar as it is supported by objective details, objective considerations and thoughts. And it is a fleeing from the truth insofar as a person can never give himself over to that which is objective in a wholly unprejudiced way, insofar as thinking always bends, to an extent, with his life.

We can also say in a religious form, all seeking for a worldview is, in the deepest sense, always a seeking after God. Above every worldview hang the words once written by Paul of the heathen world, "that they should seek God, and perhaps feel their way toward him and find him" [Acts 17:27]. A human being needs God, his whole soul asks after God, and outside God his seeking and thinking cannot find any peace. And thus, every worldview ends in God. It is an approaching toward the power of God; it is carried and compelled by a longing for God. Conversely, it is equally applicable to every worldview that it is a fleeing from God, a pulling back from God, a not daring to accept God, because all recognition of God is a judgment of self. Finding God always means losing self. And thus, all seeking always pulls back. We can say, every person seeks God, and we can also say, there is no one who seeks God. No one dares to give himself over fully. That complete self-denial lies beyond human capacities.

Each worldview is a living proof of that notable discord that abides in the human soul. A human being does not rise above it. This is because the relationship between the human being and God is always awry. Sin's delicate poison has sunk into all his powers and desires. A human being cannot do other than both seek God, because he longs for him in the deepest part of his being, and evade him, because he fears and hates him with every fiber of his being.

It is precisely this [dynamic] that makes the battle of the worldviews so great and wondrous. It is not a cozy discussion. It always contains tension and depth. In his worldview, a person often approaches God— the highest truth—more closely than he expresses through his life. Life is so clumsy and so heavy, so difficult to push and to move onto a different path. Life itself is much more godless than thinking is. In [the act of] considering, the longing for God can express itself much more tenderly and beautifully than in the rough material of hard, daily experience. Therefore, the struggle is much more refined and subtle here. It stirs the emotions to see that from all the ancient eras to the present day, almost every deeply thought-out worldview ascends toward God and ends in God. Then one feels, first, what is felt so little in life, that the urge toward God has taken hold of us much more strongly than we ourselves often think. That they might feel and find him [Acts 17:27]!

But even there, in that seeking, in that thinking about God, when listening to him, and actually fleeing him time and time again, evading him in the semblance of seeking him, how very much the human being hides a discord within himself and how very much he wants what he does not want and seeks what he cannot seek are all the more starkly [seen].

Now that we have sketched out these thoughts in broad strokes, we must move our investigation over into concrete [terms] and thus pursue these different elements in the struggle [between] worldviews. Naturally, we cannot possibly tackle every worldview one by one and must limit ourselves to a few prominent sorts. That is also enough, however, to show how rich a thing it is to possess a worldview. The great danger in our age is precisely our fear of worldviews. People are tired of asking questions and skeptically turn away from each worldview with the doubt and reluctance [that asks], "What is truth?" [John 18:38].

May hunger for the truth fill us, doubtless because of the truth itself but also because the truth must be the foundation our life rests on and must set us free from ourselves. Whoever believes and does the truth will be free.

2

The Essence of Personality

BEFORE WE CAN MOVE our investigation of the connection between personality and worldview further forward, we need to try to form our own impression of the essence of personality. It goes without saying that we can do this only briefly because the difficulties here are so many that each detailed investigation would take us much too far away from our goal.

Now it is indeed good that we place something in the foreground that might easily otherwise go unnoticed, namely, the idea that we understand so painfully little of the life of the soul and all that goes with it. Whenever we point out a few of its greatest functions and phenomena with words, it perhaps seems in many regards like a well-ordered whole, and it might perhaps seem that we are all quite well engaged with the problems. That, however, would be a sad illusion. The more deeply we think about it, [the more we see that] the soul with all its phenomena is such an incomprehensible puzzle to us that we often feel overcome by the desire no longer to probe its depths. Actually, each concept is a mystery; we use words such as *soul, function, consciousness, I,* and many more like them. We also know [*weten*] what we understand by them, but the correct insight into the essence of [these] things will always be denied to us. That is so with regard to the simple psychical phenomena, but it counts in a much stronger sense for the more complicated, foundational problems.

Nonetheless, we must form a verdict on the complicated questions and at various points provide a description of what we mean. With regard to the concept of personality, for example, we immediately need to begin with a definition. By *personality*, we understand an organized soul that has come to consciousness of itself. When we present it as such, it seems that a personality has two aspects: organization and self-consciousness. The first mark of the personality is always [its] unity. A soul can be called a personality insofar as the powers within it have come into connection with each other and have penetrated one another. The opposite of personality is thus a soul that is full of oppositions, full of inner confusion—a chaotic, uneven soul. A second mark appears alongside this, in that a soul that has been synthesized like this must also possess a certain degree of self-consciousness. The instinctive must have stepped over into consciousness and clarity.

Immediately, we must add another definition to this: the soul is independent, created by God, with its distinctive functions found in its entire nature and essence, with strivings, capacities that we see coming to the fore in the conscious life, and with which we become acquainted from that conscious life. At the core, at the center in that soul, we call that which forms the foundation of all the psychical phenomena *I*.

At first, this all seems very difficult, but we must begin with some such formulations in order to prevent misunderstandings as far as possible—all the more in psychological investigations where misunderstandings can so easily slip in. Now, however, we must try to acquire more definition in these things. What we have noticed until now is still purely formal; it gives little insight into the accord, the content of the soul that may be considered "personality." With this, the question naturally arises, What are the psychical capacities that we come across in an organized form in the personality and that by themselves also stand chaotically alongside one another? Which elements are we dealing with that have penetrated and pervaded each other in the personality?

To answer this question, we must first give a closer account of what the soul does, of the manner in which it behaves in life. We can indeed first move toward this [understanding] when we reflect in a detailed way on the phenomena of consciousness, on all that happens in our conscious life.

In the first place, we notice that the soul possesses a great *receptive* capacity. In our conscious life, we begin to see this as we notice directly that our consciousness stands open to many impressions from the external world. It reflects the external world. The soul is receptive, which is to say, in very many regards it behaves passively and takes into itself what the external world has to say to it. The doors through which these impressions enter it from the external world are what we call the senses. You have the eye, which opens itself up to the world of visible things. It notices lines and colors. The visible world offers itself to us and makes itself known to us. Through this door—the main door, we might well call it—an overwhelming mixture of impressions comes into us, and in taking this up, our eye possesses an exceptionally great acuity and refinement. Further to this, you have the ear, which possesses a simply astonishing sensitivity for all sounds, for tones, for fine nuances in the human voice. You have the tongue and other parts of the mouth and throat, which make us conscious of taste. In short, the soul is almost always busy receiving. The world never stops influencing the soul. This is so strong that nowhere near all the impressions that rush at the soul can come to the consciousness. At this moment there are visible things that want to enter me through my eyes, sounds from the street that reach my ears, all sorts of olfactory sensations, sensations of warmth, taste, and so on that offer themselves to me. My soul is not equipped to experience all of them consciously and simultaneously in a single moment, and thus it must apply a certain selectivity. It does this in its attentiveness. I do not take in all sorts of other impressions that are present, and I focus, for example, only on the sound of the human voice that is speaking to me. But in all this, the soul is receptive. Its posture to the external world is the continuous request "Speak to me!" And the soul itself listens, receives.

In the second place, we can say of the soul that it *conserves*. We also first begin to see this in the conscious life. As soon as we go after our presuppositions, concepts, and so on, we notice that older images constantly reappear. That shows us that the soul seems to keep a firm hold on old images and that it always carefully preserves them. The soul's conserving capacity is one of the greatest secrets that it hides within itself. We do not notice that it does this or how it does it, but we see from the results that it seems to happen. The soul does this naturally. It is always doing this by virtue of its own nature, in most cases without us somehow consciously influencing it [to do so].

Now we see the conserving function of the soul coming to the fore in all sorts of different forms. We meet it, for example, in the memory. I can still repeat all sorts of series of words by heart that I learned as a boy at school. We meet it in a different way in recognition. When we see a thing, we can sometimes have a strong feeling that we have seen it before. That is also only possible when the soul seems to have retained an image of it from before. We can also observe the conserving power in remembering. Remembrance always regards our own life. I remember episodes from my early years, I can determine precisely when they happened, how I felt then, and so on. Through remembrance, we have an overview of our own history, and we keep a firm grip on our own past. Now the soul sets to work selectively in the conserving of impressions, and it holds on to some more firmly than to others. It prefers, for example, those impressions in which it is specially interested. Others, to which it was more or less indifferent, are jettisoned as quickly as possible, so as to gain as little ballast as possible. But that it does conserve is sufficiently proved from all sorts of phenomena.

With regard to these things, one more thing must be pointed out. The conserving capacity possessed by the soul is so great that the soul itself often does not know what it has buried in the cellars of the memory. All manner of old memories that it thought it had forgotten long ago can sometimes suddenly resurface in later years. They seem to have lain buried in the dusty depths of the subconscious for years and then suddenly to have been called back to life. That is a secretive occurrence that we cannot pursue in a detailed way, but one thing is indeed sure: the soul anxiously and carefully retains what has happened in the past, so that in later years it may reach a verdict on it.

The third thing that occupies us is the *connecting* power of the soul. It does not allow the older impressions and all the new impressions that present themselves to it to remain detached from each other. It always brings them into connection with one another. When I see something new, I remember that I once saw something similar; I connect them and draw a conclusion: "Oh, then this or that will happen." I see the present in the light of the past and the past in connection with the present. Actually, this is what thinking really is. Thinking is nothing other than connecting impressions, noting their relatedness, their inner relations. This can happen in all sorts of forms, in a simple manner, but sometimes also in very complex forms. You always encounter the same psychical power: the soul is never satisfied simply by setting things alongside each other. It must also know [*weten*] the connection, the link, between them. Because it looks for this, things become clearer to it the longer [it considers them]. It begins to notice that the world is full of thought, that the phenomena in the world are connected to each other.

The psychical capacity, however, is not exhausted by this [connecting]. After all, everything is still objective. The soul goes further and lives its own subjective life. This means that it also steps *appreciatively* into the reality beyond itself. It says, "I find that red color beautiful"; "I do not like that combination of tones." It always makes value judgments. It says, "I like it here; I find this room cozy, tasteful." It judges, "I find this person kind; another irritating, hateful." It does not move through life like a dead thing; rather, it is bound to the world outside itself by all manner of fine bonds of sympathy, preference, and taste. It does all this naturally. It is a power within itself that it uses naturally in every moment.

It stamps everything with a certain value, be that for good or ill. It enjoys the sun, the light, the majesty of an autumnal scene. The world speaks to it, as though [the soul] is drawn into it. And by what standard does it judge those things? According to its inner norms. It has this balance in its own hands; its own needs are the standard that it lays down for those things. It is always moved by things, sometimes in an almost imperceptibly light way, but sometimes it can be engulfed by love or by hate, by rejection or appreciation.

In the last place, we can say, the soul *longs*. That is a new power within it. It does not accept the world as the things within it present themselves. Rather, it always wants to bring about changes within it. It re-forms the world according to its own taste. To [the soul], reality is still possibility, from which it can make everything. It actively intervenes in what happens. It exerts itself in influencing things as they occur. It is like a servant that receives and bows down, but it is also a king that rules and even makes his will to be done. It has ideals and pursues them, and it has desires that it seeks to fulfill. And so it advances through life and intervenes in the delicate game of everyday occurrences.

You will admit that we encounter quite a sum of powers in the soul. Passive, in receiving and appreciating, but also active, in connecting and longing. There are those that remain hidden within a person, in conserving and thinking. There are also those that move outward, in the great willing that is rooted in longing. The soul is so wondrously multifaceted that you can barely imagine its richness adequately. It is a fine tool that is suitable for everything, that hides a world of diversity within itself. Only when you can see and imagine that, can you understand and wonder at it.

When we see all these functions more closely, we notice that this multifaceted [nature] can also be the cause of its discord. The external world works its influence on us through the receptive function, and we [exercise our influence] on the external world through the will. It is possible that these two come into conflict and that tension and opposition can exist between them. The inward functions can be disturbed and limited by the [functions] that are directed outward: receiving and willing. In short, the multifaceted nature of the soul can lead to contrast, to an inner struggle, to difficulties. In *personality* we understand a soul within which those different functions balance each other out, in which a certain synthesis is found.

This becomes increasingly clear when we take account of the manner in which the soul tends to behave in the practice of life. Directly from this, [we know] that the different functions do not just sit adjacently to each other in the soul. Rather, they penetrate one another; they mingle into each other. It would take us too far [off course] to work this out broadly here. As such, it should suffice to remark that willing plays a role in thinking, sensing plays a role in willing, and feeling plays a role in sensing. All the functions involve themselves in each other and work together. We can only separate them fully through logical abstraction.

All the more noticeable is that the connection within which the functions move toward each other is different for each person. From this, then, every human being's personality bears a different imprint. The accent seems to be different for each person, and it is precisely in this that we differ so wondrously from each other. I can provide only a few examples of this, of course, to clarify my meaning.

Imagine a person in whom all these five functions are present in a normal way but in whom, for example, the receptive function is over-grown and has pushed itself into the center of the whole, dominating all the others. You thus see a person who does indeed conserve and who also thinks and appreciates and longs but above all who takes up things within himself, receives, and listens. That person is exceptionally open to the external world, so strongly that he has almost no inner life. He lives in the external world. He must always see, hear, and receive impressions from outside. He has an insatiable hunger for impressions and is unhappy when he does not see people, things, impressions. He does not have a strong will. Actually, the things he wants are what everyone wants. He toddles along in the direction that everyone follows. That is why he constantly redefines himself when he moves into a new environment. He has a chameleonlike quality and takes on the color of his environs. Neither will you find a sense of his own taste. Rather, the things he finds beautiful are the things everyone finds beautiful, and he rejects as "stupid" the things that differ, to a certain degree, from the usual. His life is defined by the external world. He does nothing more than take up within himself what others do, what others say, and what others judge. He cannot easily provide leadership in any movement; rather, he is a born follower who moves along behind others. In terms of rigorous thinking, he is a zero. He does not live his own life but rather lets himself be determined by the world beyond himself. His life system is completely passively oriented.

Now experience teaches that in reality, such a person is nonetheless moved by other powers. The natural need for self-preservation that resides within him cannot express itself in the normal way of gaining independence [to develop] a distinct, individual life. He is too passive, too much a slave to the external world, for this. Therefore, these tendencies try to show themselves in all sorts of indirect ways. That can happen, for example, in the sense that he inclines toward greed. His ideals do not develop in the direction of being something but rather toward having something. He does not strive toward the unfolding of the capacities and gifts of his personality, but rather, he focuses himself on acquiring more and more things. As a character, he allows himself to be trampled on and molded by others as they wish, but he compensates himself for this by their small gestures [of approval toward him], with whatever he can get. You see, thus, a very typical constellation that wholly characterizes such a personality in its every trait. It goes without saying that you seldom come across such one-sided [personality] types as I have sketched here, but you will probably find people in your environment who resemble this type to a certain degree. The central aspect of their character is that all their psychical capabilities have been organized around the receptive, passive function so that this passive function has overgrown all others. The balance of the personality has been skewed and warped.

In contrast to this one-sided passive person, we can imagine another who contrasts with him in many regards: the person in whom the will, oriented toward the external world, stands at the center of life. He does not live from the outside inward but rather from the inside outward. In everything, he wants to live by his own insights, according to his own needs. And he wants to leave his mark on everything. He has a constant urge to mold his environment according to his own ideas. Listening to others and paying close attention to what others say is particularly difficult for him. He sees what he wants to see and hears what he wants to hear. His eyes and ears are employed in service of his will. He cannot take things up into himself and process them objectively. Because of this, he often brushes other people aside, without realizing sufficiently that others also have their own needs, ideals, and thoughts. Perhaps without even being aware of it, his danger is lust for power, for tyranny over his neighbor. Now this danger is the flip side of many outstanding qualities: [when moved] into a different environment, for example, he will keep his own distinct identity. His life does not remind us of the weather vane that turns with every wind. Rather, from the beginning it is marked by independence. With him, you know what you are dealing with, and you can work with him as he has some stability. Such people are also often honest, candid, and lacking in the fawning, jealous [qualities] that we see in others. They are direct. The whole psychical constellation [of such a person] is different from that of the predominantly passive person.

And yet in the seemingly independent person are often powers that work in a wholly different direction. In many cases, he is inwardly much more dependent on others than he supposes. You see this in the robust young lad who defies everything with tremendous brutishness and seems not to worry about anything. In reality, though, he pays careful attention to his classmates' applause. He is in no way indifferent to whether they cheer and follow him. In many regards, he follows the public—the public from which he desires and chases adulation.

Imagine, finally, another constellation [of traits], namely, one in which the inwardly processing functions—imagination and thinking—stand as the center point. This is the deep thinker who leads his own life, who is always more or less absent, who is directed inward. He takes part in daily existence but only in part. Midconversation, you notice that his eyes wander and that his thoughts seem to have been led to completely different things. He never participates wholeheartedly in practical life. He is always the dreamer, the philosopher. Others make jokes about his absentmindedness. In general, such people are mentally agile and easy in their interactions. That has to be so since they find nothing more awful than disagreement with others. Such is far too great a distraction; it drags them too far into the mundane worries of everyday life. In effect, they have to entrench themselves against the external world. They have to make sure that it does not influence them too much, does not occupy them very much. Their life is thus constantly arming itself against their sensations, in order to give the inner life the run of the roost.

Thus, we have a few groupings of psychical functions that are easy to find in practice. Each grouping brings with it distinctive qualities and leads to particular consequences. The question of where the balance of psychical functions lies is therefore—for our knowledge of the personality—also a very weighty one. From each one, you can easily draw in and approach the others.

Now it goes without saying that in reality all these things relate to one another in a much more complicated way than we have sketched out thus far. In the first place, there are only a few people in whom this psychical balance is so one-sidedly found in a single function. For most, there are several [functions] that form the core of the psychical system. Alongside this, among people who resemble each other with regard to the grouping of functions, there are still all sorts of differences in character, in the way their psychical capacities work. We should in no sense believe that the richness of that diversity can be expressed in a simple schema. The richness of God's thoughts is too impressive for that.

It is important, though, that we see the power of the personality in all these phenomena. The tensions that emerge unnoticed between the different functions are resolved and removed. The personality grows in a certain direction, takes on a distinct accent, a balance between the different relationships. This is of immeasurably great importance. A human being is not simply the sum total of psychical functions but rather a whole that has grown together, in which each function takes up a distinctive place and has a unique meaning. The soul is an organism, not a machine in which the functions are fixed in place like gears. As an organism, it has the right to claim the honorable name of *personality*.

[Even] when we place these things next to each other, however, we have not plumbed the depths of the soul. We should be able to say that what we have done thus far is point to a light show. We have shown how the cables run and where the lamps are and have made others notice that in each person, the cables are wired differently. That is all very important, but it gives rise to other questions: Where does the electricity come from that makes the light show come alive? It is already of great worth if we know [*weten*] that the soul *can* receive, *can* retain, bind, appreciate, and want, but now come the problems: Why does it do so? What is the force that compels it to these activities, that drives it to receive, to retain, and so forth? The fact that the soul can [do these things] absolutely does not mean that it must and really does do them. Where is the power source that provides for the whole light show, that brings the entire, complex instrument to life?

The motor [driving] the whole enterprise, the entirety of this wonderful light show, is hunger. At first impression, this perhaps sounds strange, but it will quickly become easier for you to imagine. Without that hunger, the soul would be a dead thing, having many capacities but without any urge to put those capacities to use. Now, however, [the soul] does set to work. It throws itself at the world. All the functions and powers rooted in it are set to work.

The sort of hunger that this is, to which we must pay attention, is difficult to describe at length. In the first place, we can call it the hunger for self-preservation, for self-cultivation, for self-maintenance. From the beginning onward, it hides within the human being and works within him like a motor. That motor sets in motion the refined powers of perception. That person will regard the world, studying it in order to find the necessary elements for his existence within that world. That hunger drives him into society. He looks to progress within it, asks for honor, value, recognition, a place to develop, possibilities to cultivate his gifts. That hunger influences his thinking, feeling, and willing. He feels downcast when someone works against him, does not understand him, aggrieves him. He strives for progress. That hunger can also reveal itself in all manner of ways and in all sorts of forms. It can be shown in pride, in ambition, in a need to be praised. It can be revealed in passivity, in self-pity, in the thought that you have been dealt a very poor hand by nature. The human being can feel like a hero who can do anything and dares to, like a saint who is actually too good for this world, like a victim who always faces adversity and misery, like a martyr who is opposed by all. Through the entire character, you find the slender off-shoots of this deep and basic instinct. It drives a person, it inspires him, it makes him grasp hold of the world, of life. It makes him feel that he must work at all things, that his life's happiness is at stake.

In the second place, we can point to the hunger for conviviality, for sympathy, friendship, love. The human being is a convivial, social being who naturally seeks contact with others. In the early childhood years, you especially find the connection to father and mother, later to friends, then girlfriends and boyfriends, and later still, this ripens into true love. In all these relationships, it is a matter of sympathy, friendship, and love, with all the differences in form and manner, because of the need for *Wirbildung* [the cultivation of *we*], for fellowship, for a losing of yourself into a higher *we*. This need is also worked into all psychical functions. The human being looks to get to know another, to be atten-tive to him, to think about him. The human being seeks another, to form a bond, and he feels happy in his love. All the powers of the soul are set in motion, as it were, by this motor, its receptivity, retention, thinking, feeling, and wanting. Again, this social instinct distinguishes itself in a multiplicity of expressions, desires, and sentiments. It can lead to sympathy, mercy, friendliness, self-denial, the need to serve, to help, to support. With all these, however, the deepest sense of being one with your neighbor stands at the foreground: if he suffers, so do we; if he rejoices, we rejoice with him.

All these powers first come to their highest and purest development in strong love. There we indeed have a *Wirbildung*, two individuals becoming one: a sharing of priorities, of needs, of struggle and of vic-tory, of longing, of disappointment, in short, of all the things of life. A marriage that brings this fellowship into practice, that rests in that fellowship, enriches and ennobles a person because—and this is what it is primarily about—the individual, being an individual, is indeed one part of our existence, even a very important part of it, but it is far from everything. We are just as much members of a fellowship, a moment in a greater "*Wir*" [we], a part of a more comprehensive whole.

In the third place, we must point to the hunger for God. Because of the nature of the subject, this is more difficult to approach and is also harder to know [*kennen*], but a deeper consideration of history quickly brings us onto the right path. We especially come to know this hunger of the soul negatively. The human being shows that although he has that which is visible, finite, and temporary, the deepest part of his soul is not satisfied. He remains incomplete, and the greatest creations of culture are not equipped to take away this incompleteness forever. There seems to be something in the human being that sees more, that wants [something] higher, that cannot rest until it has found the invisible, the infinite, the eternal. Where this need comes from, we can leave alone for the time being. History simply shows us this fact. It is a fact that all peoples have reached higher, have sought the eternal, [have sought] God, and that their whole lives have pointed to that seeking.

This deeply rooted impulse in the human soul also sets to work on all the delicate functions and powers like a motor. It stimulates his observations. The human being goes into the world taking note of what points him to God, of what brings him closer to God. It excites his thinking. The human being reaches higher in his thoughts and wants to approach God in his thoughts. He plays along in his feelings; he feels tired, unsatisfied when God feels far from him; and he feels enriched and deepened when he lives near to God. Finally, this impulse influences the life of his will. He serves God, and through all sorts of actions, he tries to come closer [to him]. In short, his life is marinated in a deep and indelible desire for fellowship with God. With one person, that will work more strongly in his intellectual functions, with another in the emotional or practical functions, according to the balance found in that personality, but the need is common to all.

This is [how it is] seen from the human side. From God's side, it corresponds to his revelation, his speaking to the human being, his making himself known, and his approach to the heart and the mind.

As regards the human being, it is clear that "being an individual" is only one side of his existence, albeit an important one. The fullness of his existence, however, is not expressed in it [because] he is more than that. He is also a creature of God, can only be known and understood in relation to God, and stands in an everlasting relationship to the eternal one.

Having pursued this threefold impulse in the human soul, we see that the functions and capabilities of the soul are moved by powerful motors. The human is compelled; his life feels impulses; his longings [receive] content; his feeling [receives] standards from that deeper, fundamental tendency. His whole psychical existence is set to work.

In principle, these three great tendencies have no need to oppose each other. They can stand alongside one another in perfect harmony. The human being is not only an individual, but he is also an individual. He is not only part of a fellowship, but he is nonetheless a part of a fellowship. He does not only live in God, but he still lives and moves in God. All three express a side of his existence, and as such, all three are justified. He may strive for self-maintenance, and this striving does not have to exclude or hinder his impulse toward fellowship. The three great tendencies that move his life and give direction apply themselves to each other. And as such, we can conceive of a delicate, subtle balance between these three. It is conceivable that they would be perfectly equally weighted in a human soul and that they would be in harmony with one another—so that [this person] is not too much of an individual and not too little of a social being but rather that everything is united in a striking manner. The issue is the balance between these three deep, foundational powers.

But while that is conceivable, in practice we see that it does not exist. The balance within the human being is askew—it lies absolutely to one side. Above all, this shows us that he is far too much an individual; he strives far too strongly for self-maintenance, self-development, self-enrichment, and lives too little as a social being. He pushes his neighbor to the side, does not think about how his neighbor suffers or is pained. He looks too strongly only at himself. The longing for God that is rooted in his nature remains weak. It wields little influence on the practice of his life. One [of the powers] is brought too far to the foreground, and the other two are shoved into a corner. The human being has a threefold love: he must love God as the highest Being, as the ground on which he is rooted; he must love his neighbor; and [he must love] himself. This threefold love must merge into a complete harmony, without any one canceling out the others. In practice, though, we see that this connection, this harmony, is broken. One [of the powers] overwhelms the other two and pushes them both to the side.

That is the secretive phenomenon that we designate "committing sin." Sin is the disruption of the personality. It is the breaking of this harmony. Sin is this: that these three great tendencies, which do not naturally exclude one another, come into conflict with each other and stand in opposition to each other. And because the motor is running defectively and does not work properly, the whole psychical system, with all its functions and powers, is pushed in the wrong direction.

Nevertheless, although his soul is full of contrasts, although everything is awry and twisted, the human being tries to come to a synthesis. He tries to join the broken pieces together into a unity; he tries to reconcile the discords into a higher synthesis. From the great mosaic that is his soul, he tries to form a harmonious whole—although one color is used far too much, and the unity is spoiled. That is no longer easy. In actual fact, it cannot be done, considering the deep discords that tear his life apart. But he tries to do it nonetheless. He chases it. It is precisely these great polarities, precisely the shrill contrasts, that push him all the more strongly to strive for unity. To become a personality, to be [a personality], is his task, his ideal. He strives for the impossible: the organization, the synthesis of the contorted.

To be a personality is thus not something that is given to the human being. Rather, it is something he pursues. It is not what the Germans call a *Gabe* [gift] but rather an *Aufgabe* [predisposition toward a duty]. Now you could still ask, "But how is it that a person ends up striving for that organization? In what does that organizing tendency, which compels him toward personality, rest?"

We must then descend deeper into the cellars of the soul, to that which lies behind all those functions and tendencies, to the *I*. The human being is an *I*, which is to say, there is a unity within him that carries all these functions and in which these tendencies rest. That is the very deepest thing. It is his self. Despite all the contrast [within him], it is one *I* that lies at the foundation of everything. The unity of that *I* is the thing that works through all the layers of his psychical existence, that wants to add all the phenomena together into a synthesis. Unity is given in the center. That unity of the center works outward from there toward the periphery. The human being is an *I*, and therefore, at the core is already a personality. But he must now become this in his appearance, in his revelation to the external world. In potential, the human being is a unity, but he must now become this in actual terms—he must become it in practice, with all his contrasts. "Being a personality" is in a certain sense a *Gabe* [gift], insofar as the person is born as a potential unity, as an *I*, but in another sense it is an *Aufgabe* [predisposition] insofar as the person who must pursue it must also realize that unity in his life. The one does not shut out the other. Rather, it demands and assumes the other.

In all this, we have discussed only one mark of the personality, namely, its unity and organization. There is another mark, namely, self-consciousness, but we want to treat this with more brevity. The concept of *personality* presupposes a certain degree of self-consciousness.

On this point it must be understood not only that the human being *is* something but also that he *knows* [*weet*] that he is something, and not only that he *does* something but that he *knows* that he does it. In different psychical actions (among others, remembering, thinking, wanting), this self-consciousness is not simply an accompaniment. It is, rather, an unmissable condition [for those actions]. Again, the degree and manner of self-consciousness varies greatly in every person, but it can be taken for granted that self-consciousness is a prerequisite for "being a personality." As he reveals his life, a person who acts purely by intuition—who lives only intuitively and does not know what he is doing or what he is—might display many fine features, but he nonetheless lacks the intentionality, the deliberateness, and, because of this, the continuous clear outline that we might expect from a personality. To move more deeply into this matter, however, would take us too far offtrack, and as such, we must content ourselves with these few remarks on it.

Whenever we consider these things in their connections, we can immediately understand that we must be able to find a close link between personality and worldview. Actually, nothing else is imaginable, and experience also shows that it is demonstrable.

From the concept of *personality*, we can already establish a few lines *a priori*, to which we will later return for closer inspection. In the first place, though, worldviews will express the extent to which their creators were personalities. You can see the extent of their organization, of their inner synthesis, reflected in their worldviews. Someone who is a powerful personality, who lives consciously from his unity, who has found a synthesis in his soul or at least has approached that synthesis, will give expression to that same unity in his worldview. In one way or another, he will be inclined toward monism; he will see the world as a synthesis, as a unity, just as he has found the same such thing in himself. And conversely, in one way or another, in his worldview, the person who lives from contrast, who has not reconciled the inner oppositions and who sees no opportunity to do so, will lean on dualism. The world does not allow itself to be thought of and summarized as a unity. It is full of discord: this thing [against] that thing, one thing [versus] another. As such, we can see worldviews through the concept of unity and, through this, see degrees of personality reflected [in them].

In the second place, in a person's worldview, we are able to explore which psychical function is primarily active in his life. The person who conserves and thinks and wants but who receives and appreciates above all will doubtless seem to show that functional balance in his worldview. The different functional groupings will be reflected, so to speak, in these worldviews. Their one-sidedness will be expressed in these worldviews and thus will give rise to conflicts. This is also fairly obvious. It is inconceivable that it would be any other way.

In the third place, a worldview will reveal itself to the extent that the person is conscious of being an individual and a social being at the same time and to the extent that he knows [*kent*] God and loves God. That moral balance will make itself known involuntarily in his worldview and will define his relationship to himself, to his fellow human, to God. It is not necessary for a person's worldview to represent precisely what he is in his life. As a rule, as we have already seen, someone's worldview is usually better than his life is. Nonetheless, that inner posture will come to expression more or less unconsciously in his worldview. Thinking can never distance itself so far from life because both are rooted in the same personality.

It is in this threefold way that a personality will be reflected to a greater or lesser degree in a worldview: in the first place, in the unity, the extent of the synthesis, and the organization; in the second place, in the functional balance (Which psychical function do you consider central? Which action do you set as the middle point?); in the third place, in the moral balance (How do you think about the relationship between one person and another, between human beings and God?).

Finally, a single observation: In this chapter, we have reproduced the different lines in a schema. The danger of such a schema is always that you quickly think you now know [how things are], that you imagine yourself to have understood life in dry and arid terms. In the very least, that is so. Let us finish, then, with the same thought that we proposed at the beginning: the more deeply we think about the reality of the life of the soul, the more we end up with puzzles. We can draw a few lines, but the great questions of what consciousness, soul, and the *I* are; how it is possible that such contrasts live within a human being; in short, the actual fundamental questions, are always ones that we must answer with a *non liquet* [it is not clear]. Here everything is so inwardly interwoven, and we can only stare at it in amazement. In that regard, may all shallow rationalism be far from us. We want to let the mysteries of the soul remain in their great beauty and not to disguise our ignorance toward those mysteries for a single second.[1]

---

1   Compare this entire chapter with my *Inleiding in de zielkunde* (Kampen: J. H. Kok, 1926). In the current short chapter, I have revised a few points that seemed to give rise to misunderstandings, in order to make my meaning clear.

The Problem of Unity

THE SAME QUESTION confronts every great thinker: To what extent can the phenomena in the world be reduced to a comprehensive unity? May we say that the universe in which we live and in which such an unimaginable number of contrasts comes to the fore can be thought of as a unity? That question will necessarily impose itself on each person who applies his mind to the problems of world and life. Thinking [itself] compels us toward it, asks about that unity, strives for that unity. And not only thinking—the personality itself is the thing that must move in this direction. It is always from this that we find the effort to view the world monistically in the struggle between worldviews and to lay bare its phenomena as parts of one organic whole. At first, this means encountering much diversity, although that diversity quickly allows itself to be reduced to different main groups, until finally, none of the unity [that was first] sought remains. Now it is clear that it is not equally easy to find that unity everywhere. Indeed, there are very many worldviews that actually never even approach it. For everyone who has some sense of the deep contrasts that we must deal with in life, of the contrasts through which life moves, this phenomenon is not in the least surprising. The world in which we live can always give rise to the thought that it is dualistic in essence. From antiquity, that dualism has played an important role in the history of worldviews.

If you wish to form an impression of these things, we can proceed from *animism*, which is the form of religion, for example, that we encounter in a number of peoples in our [Dutch East] Indies. Animism has this idiosyncrasy: it presents all things as animate; it believes in a sort of soul matter that does not only reside in the human being but also fills all other beings. A tree, a waterfall, a crater, a river, an animal—in short, all the beings that we deal with—are animate, and in them reside spirits and powers. In this way, the spiritual and the natural merge into one. The human being projects his own considerations and intentions into the things that surround him, and in this way he acquires a very simple picture of the world. The damaging workings that proceed from many things are known by the spirits that inhabit them, [for which reason] the spirits are things for which we must always be on our guard. In practice, such a belief leads to all manner of idiosyncratic phenomena. Someone will try, for example, to ward off the damaging workings of the spirits by placating them, through formulas, incantations, magical means, deceptions. In general, a person becomes attached to all sorts of magical practices and expects that the workings can be influenced through various external means.

This animism is spread out among many peoples in various forms, and even long after it has been given up officially, it exercises a clearly noticeable influence on all sorts of business. The entirety of life is taken up into religion through it: birth and marriage, the building of a house, laying a garden, sickness and death, sowing and harvest, business and enterprise. Either directly or indirectly, all the things of life are seen as being influenced by spirits. Because of this, incantations and magical means play a role in every event of any significance. The whole of life is an ongoing attempt to ward off those influences or to direct them to one's own benefit. At every event and in each thing, the animist takes account of the hidden influences that are nonetheless the only real thing in reality.

When viewed more closely, it quickly seems that dualistic tendencies are at work in this animism. Namely, there are two sorts of spirits, of hidden powers: good and evil. That dualism is not ethical in character; it mostly limits itself to the contrast of suffering and success. Evil spirits are those that persecute human beings, that press them down, that mislead them, that try to ensnare them, to bring them to a fall. And to the contrary, good spirits are those, as it were, that spread blessing and joy. Because one has to pay more serious attention to the first sort, they mostly play a greater role in [one's] life, while the good [spirits] remain more or less in the background. If someone tries to portray them, the evil spirits are drawn in awful forms, while the latter [spirits] make us think of well-being and joy. In all these phenomena, we are dealing with a primitive dualism that does not actually arrive at the great, objective contrasts but rather remains at the [level of] subjective, emotional contrasts. As such, there is no talk of an attempt at reconciliation [between objective contrasts in the world]. The world is a strange, secretive whole, in which one finds a path only with much difficulty. Until the very end, it is something that must be observed with great caution.

Much deeper, more honest, and more fundamental is the dualism that was found in the ancient *Persian religions*, and that (in contrast to the [aforementioned] primitive dualism) can indeed be called "ethical dualism." This is the faith that goes back to the great thinker Zoroaster[1] and that we find laid down in the sacred Avesta texts.[2] Not everything in them is known to us yet, but we can form a clear concept of the whole from all sorts of fragments.

The god Ahura Mazda ("the very wise lord") is worshiped as the highest of all beings, the god of lights and the one who rewards all good works. He is glorified in all sorts of striking expressions and is portrayed to us as the holy, the omniscient, the judge who reveals that which was secret. Around him are good spirits. All that proceeds from him, incidentally, is joy, light, righteousness. In the fullest sense of the word, he is Most High, the only one who is worthy of worship.

---

1   Zoroaster, also known as Zarathustra, an ancient Iranian spiritual teacher and founder of what is now referred to as Zoroastrianism. There is no scholarly consensus on when Zoroaster lived.—Ed.

2   The Avesta is the principal collection of Zoroastrian religious texts.—Ed.

The good spirits that serve him, the angels who stand alongside him, all have their own task in the world.

Against this Ahura Mazda (who is also called Ormizd), the Persian religion knows a god of darkness, Angra Mainyu, "destructive spirit" (who is also called Ahriman). He stands above the world of evil demons and is the creator of all that is morally impure. He may not create anything positive. His character is limited by this contrast. He can only break apart, destroy, and warp. At first, he was not set up as a god against Ahura Mazda. He is more a being of a lower order, a sort of demon. Later, however, this evil deity was divinized more and more and made equal to the good deity. He is the eternal evil that exists alongside the light and that tries to darken the good everywhere and in every part of the universe.

This idea is particularly noteworthy in many regards, because it makes this moral contrast absolute, eternal, divine. It shows the great tear deep within this world that rips the oneness of everything apart. Ultimately, the powers and influences that are at work here are not to be brought back to unity. Unbridgeable contrasts remain. By painting things in such a way, life is sketched out to an extraordinarily strong degree as a struggle with the god of darkness. The moral contrast between love and hate, purity and impurity, that a human being feels within himself leads to a cosmic principle that explains all phenomena.

But through this, at the same time, the inner conflict is brought onto a higher plane and made absolute and irreconcilable. This idea seems to contain something attractive. It is continually seized on in later times. When Christianity eventually made its entrance into the world and all manner of philosophical movements tried to harmonize its content with pagan philosophy, it was Manichaeism[3]—grasping back toward the old contrasts—that wanted to carry that dualism into the world of Christian thought. And yet, as a religion, as a system in general, it has

---

3   Manichaeism, a religion founded in the third century AD by the Parthian prophet Mani (ca. 216–274). Its intricate dualism contrasted a spiritual world of light with an evil material world of darkness.—Ed.

satisfied few. It leaves great questions unresolved and in another regard has found the needs of personality impossible to satisfy.

However strong and weighty this moral dualism may be, it was outdone in both depth and comprehensiveness by what we could call metaphysical dualism, which exceeded it in many regards and has gained far more followers.

To acquire insight here, we will proceed from *Indian religion*. There, early on, the need for a worldview was felt, and thought on the great questions of the world came to be very highly developed. We find the oldest literature in the Vedas[4]—old, religious writings that in seed form already contain all sorts of concepts found in the later systems [of thought]. The striking feature of the Vedic writings, on the one hand, is that the different gods worshiped in India are considered different approaches from one and the same divine being. Alongside this, it is notable that they regard this world as emanating from God. This world is, as it were, a part of God, has come out of God, and is essentially no different from God himself. It is like a spark from a great fire that has been shot high above the fire but that cannot be any different from the fire itself and that must eventually fall back into it. The clear distinction between God and the world preached by Christianity from the beginning is missed entirely in the Vedic writings.

In later eras, this Veda has been explained and adapted countless times. All sorts of systems of thought, full of speculations and always leading to new consequences, have been attached to it. The highest, and in a certain sense also the deepest, are the great ideas expressed in India in the so-called Upanishads,[5] which reflect—often in very beautiful ways—on the problems of the world. The form in which they are composed is mostly that of the story of the instruction of wise teachers to pupils who desired to know more about these secrets. Those teachers educate them in a very careful way, sometimes leave the pupils waiting for years before they dare entrust to them their new ideas, are willing

4   The Vedas, a body of ancient Indian religious texts that provide the oldest scriptures in
    Hinduism.—Ed.
5   The Upanishads, late Vedic Sanskrit texts dealing with Hindu philosophy.—Ed.

to leave their pupils to plod along in misunderstanding for long periods, and wait quietly for the moment when they are mature enough
to be taught the secret itself. They offer that actual secret doctrine in
symbolic, poetic forms, in very ceremonial expressions, that doubtless
must have made a deep impression.

When you ask, "What does this Indian philosophy boil down to?"
the answer must be "In essence, it is pantheistic." It is so in the sense
that it holds on to the unity of God and the world and portrays it in a
beautiful way. It points to the oneness of the human soul with the great
being that permeates all things and from which all things have come
forth. That great being is mostly called Brahma[6] but is also called the
atman,[7] the deeper self of all things. Now, of course, the human being's
deeper self, the soul, the deepest core, is one with and concurs with the
world-atman. The deepest [part] of the soul is God.

> The one who abides in the earth and yet is distinct from the earth,
> whom the earth does not know, whose body is the earth, who rules
> the earth inwardly, he is your soul, the hidden leader, the immortal.
>
> The one who abides in all beings and yet is different from
> every being, whom no being knows, whose body is all beings,
> who rules all beings inwardly, he is your soul, the hidden leader,
> the immortal.
>
> While he himself sees, he is not seen; while he himself hears, he
> is not heard; while he himself understands, he is not understood;
> while he himself knows, he is not known. Beyond him, there is
> none who sees, who hears, who understands, who knows. He is
> your soul, the hidden leader, the immortal. Whatever happens
> from him finds sorrow.

In another place, the divinity of the human soul is even more
strongly expressed:

---

6   Brahma, the "creator" within the Trimurti—the triple deity—alongside Vishnu and
    Shiva.—Ed.
7   In Hinduism, atman refers to the self or self-existent essence.—Ed.

This is my soul (atman) in the most inner place in my heart. It is smaller than a grain of rice or a grain of barley or a grain of wheat.

This is my soul, in the most inner place in my heart. It is larger than the earth, larger than the sky above, larger than heaven, larger than the worlds.

This unity of the soul with God, of the atman, the deepest part of the human being, with the world-atman itself, took on a fixed formula in the well-known description: *tat-tvam-asi*, "thou that art."[8]

That which is extremely fine, imperceptible to our senses, that is the only thing that is real; that is the soul, thou that art!

How the unity of the soul and God was further proposed, whether the soul was considered a part of the world-atman, or even as the world-atman itself, cannot occupy us for any longer. The fact is that the Upanishads are profoundly permeated with that unity itself.

Now you might respond, "But when someone adheres to this idea, at the very least, that person relies on the foundation of dualism." In a certain sense, that is correct. As a philosophical system, Indian philosophy is strongly monistic in that it unites God and world. Nonetheless, the application of this in life is always more or less permeated with dualistic principles.

This begins when you ask, "What is the way of salvation?" The answer sounds like this: "The human being must pull back from the world, must reflect in silence on the puzzles of existence, must turn inward toward himself, to his atman, and when he does that, he also finds God in that atman. The human being must turn his back on this confusing world of sensory impressions and find the path to the world-atman in the depths of his soul." On its own, this idea casts life under a dualistic shade. It brings two great features into life that are, as it were, opposed

---

8 This Sanskrit expression is often repeated in chap. 6 of the Chandogya Upanishad and deals with the relationship between the individual and the absolute.—Ed.

to one another—the material world, with all its deception, and the soul, which is one with the world-atman. The human being must move away from one and toward the other if he wants to find rest and blessedness. It is from this that the hermit's life, the fleeing from society, has expanded so greatly in every age in India. To become indifferent to all the things of life, to free yourself from love and hate, to meditate quietly on the great questions of the world, and through this to come to insight on the nature and the essence of his atman is the only way that stands open to salvation.

From this, there are indeed different questions to be posed, which have been answered in different ways in the progression of history in India. One can ask, "Why must the human being reject the material world? Is it not also from God? Why is the material world less worthy?" There are some who have answered, "The material world is eternal, is of a wholly different nature from the soul, and has a different origin. Both worlds, matter and spirit, stand, as it were, eternally against one another." When one writes it up like this, it becomes clear that the connection of soul and matter is, in fact, something unnatural, that for the soul its link to matter is a sort of dungeon, and that one must immediately wish to break that link. It is then clear that the soul must strive to be liberated from matter and must thus turn away from the world. Death cannot help in that process. Death is an apparent separation of soul and body, but the soul returns to the earth in another body. Only when it is mature, when it has completed the path of salvation, can it eternally flee the clutches of this material world.

An entirely different doctrine has found much more support in India, that of the Vedanta,[9] which found an eminent advocate in the great thinker Çankara[10] (fl. ca. 800 BC). He gave prominence [to the claim] that this material world is nothing other than a dream. It does not exist, but rather, we dream it. It is a mighty work of deception, a

9   The Vedanta, one of the six schools of Hindu philosophy.—Ed.
10 Çankara, a prominent ninth-century BC commentator on the Vedanta.—Ed.

delusion, that holds us prisoner. We think that there is a world beyond ourselves. We desire, love, hate, are worried, are afraid, and in reality we are nothing but the products of our own imagination. The inner reality is our atman, and this atman is one with the world-atman. That deception is known as maya[11] in the Indian thought world:

Just as one watches a dream or an infatuation,
　　just as one regards a fata morgana,[12]
so appears this world,
　　to him taught in the Vedanta.

Elsewhere, it is said,

That which one thinks he sees, when awake and moving
　　round the surface of the earth, as beasts and birds, and insects,
　　　　exists nowhere but in his mind;
Thus is all that his eye sees,
　　only an illusion, a waking dream.

You can sense it: the whole of his way of thinking is dualistic. Our existence must pay heed to two poles: matter and spirit. The first is delusion, a mere semblance, a dream, maya; the second is the only reality. The human being must try all the more to escape the grip of maya and enter the depths of the atman. This is how his life is approached dualistically. He must reject life, love, and hate, all the things that occupy and interest him, and draw himself back into isolation, the thoughtful approach toward the eternal atman.

It is interesting to follow how dualism is awakened all over the world, how everywhere, among people groups, the intuition arises that this world has been torn, that the phenomena cannot be completely brought back to unity, that life is full of contrast, of jarring contradiction.

11　In Hindu philosophy, maya refers to the misconception of reality.—Ed.
12　A fata morgana, a mirage.—Ed.

The Greek thinkers also came to similar dualistic conclusions, although in general they were more sober, more organized, and also more deeply penetrated by the reality of the material world. In particular, Plato[13] provided a classical formulation of the contrasts in question. He certainly weighed up the contrast of spirit and matter, though in his philosophy this took on a deeper spiritual, moral value.

The reason for this is that in his view, the soul is something wholly particular and idiosyncratic in distinction to the material world. It also comes into being in a special way, in a deliberate act by the one who formed the world. Before coming into the world, the human soul first lived in the world of ideas, where it enjoyed the highest spiritual goods and possessed direct fellowship with God. It fell, however, from that estate, moved over into evil, and, as a consequence of this, as a punishment, it was imprisoned in matter. For [the soul], this is an indescribably awful thing. It can never feel fully at home in that material world.

[And of course,] how could it? [The soul,] which once looked on the wisdom of all things in the elevated world of eternal ideas, must now—according to its birth in a body—content itself with the dull, external semblance of things. It sits bound, with its back toward the light, as though captive in a cave, and sees on the wall opposite it the shadows of things it formerly knew in reality.[14]

[The soul,] which once stood before God's countenance, is now cast down into a world that remembers only his glory from far away. It is true that [the soul] casts itself with all its energy and full devotion on that illusory world, and it is true that it grabs hold of sensible things with both hands and also often thinks it has grasped the most elevated things in that sensible world. [Nonetheless,] often, in its tiresome journey, it receives the vague memory that it once tasted much greater pleasures, that it once gazed into the deepest grounds [of all things]. It is never fully satisfied. It also never understands. With its

13 Plato (ca. 429–347 BC), the ancient Greek philosopher.—Ed.
14 Here Bavinck refers to the famous cave analogy found in Plato's *Republic*.—Ed.

understanding, it can indeed analyze and describe the relationships, the external circumstances of things, but it never approaches the essential, the deepest essence. And that dissatisfaction becomes greater and more steadfast to the degree that it more often and more honestly gives itself to the mysterious memory of the utterly glorious realm of eternal observation that continues to live on very faintly and vaguely.

Therefore, the deepest sentiment within the human being is that of homesickness for what it once possessed, before his birth in a body. Thus, the highest form of knowing [kennen] is the intuition grounded in the "memory" that takes one back from the mere semblance to the essence. The soul is lost, lost in a world where it does not belong, where it can perhaps entertain itself for a moment with the tinsel of false knowledge, but where it is not satisfied in the long run. It is imprisoned, captive in a world that can never please its deepest needs, for which reason it gasps with longing for the world of the ideas, for God's nearness.

Platonism accepts this dichotomy as one of the most essential elements of human existence. Matter and spirit, semblance and essence, shadow and idea stand opposite one another. The soul can never forget its great fall.

Without a shadow of a doubt, this system contains a great prophetic earnestness, and it is also no surprise that it has indeed become deeply ingrained in the many thinkers who came after it. Above all, the mystics of later eras have almost all oriented themselves, with greater or lesser clarity, toward Plato.

In ancient Greece, these concepts took effect in seed form. Neoplatonism portrayed life and the world in different forms but according to the same schema. Through its great philosopher Plotinus,[15] Alexandrian Neoplatonism in particular contributed a great deal to the development of these ideas. Typical of this Greek mysticism, in the first place, is the uniting of the moral contrast of good and evil with the contrast between matter and spirit. Matter is the thing that incarcerates, is

15 Plotinus (ca. AD 205–270), the founder of Neoplatonism.—Ed.

evil, or at least is the root of evil; matter is the hindrance of the higher functions, and through this, it is the lead that weighs down the eagle of the soul in its flight.

A second typical feature is that it sees in reason that which is characteristic of spirit. In essence and intention, it is rationalistic. Salvation is coming toward insight. Reasoning is above passions [and the] instincts of the lower soul; [it is] entering into perfect knowledge [kennis]. This highest knowledge [kennis] is described especially as intuition, as an observing, as "remembering." From this viewpoint, one feels naturally compelled toward the ascetic, toward world flight, toward despising life.

The essential elements of this mysticism have also permeated more recent Western [culture] through all sorts of narrow channels. And it has indeed worked fruitfully there. It has attracted the most noble minds and called powerful movements into life. This more recent Western mysticism is a remarkable collection of different tendencies. Its foundation sits on a Christian base layer, for which reason it also avoids all manner of ideas of pagan origin. It is "Christ mysticism" and sets the suffering Master in the center of its meditations. Nonetheless, it has undergone great and enduring influence from the Platonic system. Since we will later return to this Christian mysticism, a few comments will suffice at this point. You can see these Platonic foundations clearly from [several] different features.

In the first place, [we see it] in that also here, in Christian mysticism, the contrast of matter and spirit is considered more or less dualistically. Matter, the body, is sin's terrain; spirit is the power toward that which is higher, carrying the person into eternity. In practice, this leads to [the view] that one sins, above all, in the body. The sins of unchastity, of immorality, the moral passions are considered the sins *par excellence*. This is, as it were, the primordial evil and receives all the emphasis. And by contrast to it, other sins, such as insincerity, vain ambition, gossip, hatefulness, and so on, are more or less placed in the background. "Flee sensual sins, and live the life of the spirit, of the higher reason that is called to look on that which is eternal."

Now in itself, that is already the reason that some are inclined toward asceticism. The highest ideal is fleeing from the world with all its temptations, withdrawing yourself from the hustle and bustle of life in order to meditate alone on the most elevated of things. There are two spheres, the sphere of natural life, with its passions [and] attractions, and [the sphere] of the supernatural, the eternal. To be a true follower of Christ, one must leave behind the former in order to gain the latter.

Clearly, it is not the case that these foundational, dualistic ideas were equally strongly applied everywhere. By no means were all the mystics of the Middle Ages influenced by them to the same degree, although something of it resonated in the entirety of that age's way of thinking. Its traces are also unmistakable in art. Medieval art is averse to all realism. It is symbolic. It paints golden skies, ascending lines, overly slim figures. It is like a song that constantly repeats the *sursum corda*—"Lift up your hearts!"—in different forms.

Now when we consider all these different forms of dualism more closely, we immediately feel that we are dealing with the confessions of a human soul. It is the human soul that intuits, on the one hand, that it must become a personality, a unity, but on the other, that it experiences all the more that the clash, the disturbing contrast within it, is unconquerable. It resigns itself to this dichotomy, gives up on ever arriving at a synthesis, and confesses its powerlessness. Goethe[16] once provided a famous articulation of this mood:

In me there are two souls, alas, and their
Division tears my life in two.
One loves the world, it clutches her, it binds
Itself to her, clinging with furious lust;
The other longs to soar beyond the dust
Into the realm of high ancestral minds. (*Faust*)[17]

---

16 Johann Wolfgang von Goethe (1749–1832), the celebrated German poet and playwright, widely considered the greatest German writer of the modern era.—Ed.

17 Johann Wolfgang von Goethe, *Faust: Part One*, trans. David Luke (Oxford: Oxford University Press, 1987), lines 1112–21.—Ed.

We are a dichotomy, and despite all our jittering efforts, we never succeed at becoming a unity, a personality.

Because of this, we should state immediately that in a few different respects, such a dualistic worldview should not be considered unimaginable. When we unite the contrast that we experience inwardly with the great contrast of the true being and the speculation, the maya, the semblance (India), or being carried back to god (Persia), or rest in the contrast of spirit and matter (Platonism), we have then made [the contrast] absolute and eternal. We have then permanently distanced ourselves from the ideal of personality. The human being sees the flaw in his own soul as a small part of the great tear that rips straight through the world, through all the things of the world. And at the very moment he does so, he loses the ideal [of personality] itself, because from that moment on, the contrast has become uncrossable.

Dualism disjoints personality. It pulls personality further apart, piece by piece. It tears the human soul into pieces.

This is therefore all the more dangerous because in this dualism we have also pardoned the contrast within ourselves. We can no longer do anything about it. We suddenly become such sad beings who belong to two spheres set against one another, and we cast the guilt for the contrast on the world or on God. If this is indeed what we are, how could we ever reconcile the heterogeneous elements from which we are composed? We have two lives, and those two lives will never become one. That is not our own fault, our responsibility. Rather, it has many deeper causes; it is grounded in the absolute and eternal contrast. Therefore, the dualistic worldview also weakens the power of moral exertion, and it robs the human being of the ideal of personality. When you see these things, you immediately sense that the sound our worldview makes is not indifferent. Personality itself is a high-stakes game. Dualism confesses dichotomy, turns that dichotomy into a cosmic power, and accepts that dichotomy.

From this, then, [it follows] that on the basis of dualism, salvation is possible only through world flight. We must rid ourselves of a part of our essence: the natural. We must once again find unity by utterly denying a portion of our being. To withdraw yourself from the world, from life, from the material sphere, is the only possibility that remains open. But then, [if you do so,] you will never become a personality.

Dualism has always attracted many of the most outstanding minds, and who would be surprised at this? It is the admission of an honest person, a person who experiences and confesses the jarring contrast within himself. But as a worldview, it destroys personality and pours scorn on the greatest calling that we have in our lives. It creates no heroes, no people who gird themselves in the struggle of life to throw their full moral weight into the battle. It leaves the world to the world, the semblance [of things] to the semblance [of things]. It creates a spiritual aristocracy that breaks loose from all ties and entertains itself in solitude with the eternal.

Now among the monistic worldviews there are also forms that pose grave dangers to the life of the personality. For the time being, we cannot explore these deeply. We do need to point out[, however,] two forms to which we must pay special attention: in the first place, pantheistic monism, and alongside this, a monism that is more theistic.

The first places things next to one another, in a certain sense. It says,

In nature we find sun and shadow, light and dark. These certainly form a contrast, but it is a contrast that can be atheistically justified as necessary, indispensable. If there were no light, the darkness would not be beautiful or useful. Now there are both light and dark, and we think these two are beautiful together. Nature needs them both, each fulfills its task, and one cannot be thought of without the other. It is precisely the shadows that make the landscape so beautiful. The mingling of light and dark creates the sheen that neither could possibly bring on its own.

In the world, we find life and death. Those certainly form a contrast. But that contrast is also necessary, indispensable. Plants and trees die, their fallen leaves rot on the ground, but it is precisely through this that the earth is made fruitful as the fat layer that will give rich crops to future soil. In nature, death is just as necessary an element as life. Life could not exist without death. The things that rotted and were consumed in the past offer the first possibility of life to new things that will live.

In life, we find suffering and joy, failure and success, but these also belong together. Suffering is often in service of the good; it ennobles and lifts up, while all too often, success makes us superficial and lazy. The greatest deeds were all born of suffering. Suffering is of the highest importance in life. We cannot imagine it away and actually would not wish to do so.

In world history, we see good and evil, love and hate, greed and self-sacrifice. Those certainly form a contrast, but they still belong together. It is precisely this dichotomy that gives history such depth, excitement, tragedy. Events bring relief. Struggle often makes great things possible. The good becomes the great and also ends up much better, precisely through evil. All sorts of virtues—inclinations toward forgiveness, sorrow, conversion, mercy—first come about not just through good but through evil. A world history without evil would be monotonous, wholly crude, without texture and without depth. Evil is necessary in the world, necessary so that good will win, to bring it to a greater intensity and to give the whole its dramatic structure.

In other words: seen from on high, judged from the viewpoint of contemplation, good and evil are equally necessary. Together, they form a mighty drama. All the evil, the darkness, the death, the suffering, and the sin are justified, atheistically. We feel that these two are irreconcilable only because our ability to rise to the heights of that atheistic viewpoint is so poor. The semblances [of things] contrast, but in reality they are dissonances that are indeed painful for a moment but that are resolved, in a higher sense, in a wonderful harmony. In that whole, both are necessary for its powerful composition.

By painting these things so, monism deprives us of the painful feeling of contrast. It lifts us up to a new viewpoint—the atheistic—from which it shows us the harmony of things that seemed to be in conflict. In a certain sense, this reconciles life and the world in that it makes

us understand that this world is not a meaningless whole or a confusing chaos. Rather, [it shows] that other ways of viewing [life and the
world] are possible, which give us a broader overview. Because of this,
this worldview invariably charms [many]. To remain in the dichotomy
is exceptionally difficult for us. [In monism], though, we receive a
perspective that shows us that this dichotomy is needed, yes, even
necessary, and therefore also glorious.

And yet, upon closer examination, great dangers immediately come
into view. This way of seeing [life and the world] provides great difficulties for the personality. It does not save us from evil, but rather, it
simply places good and evil together, leaving them to stand alongside
one another as equally justified. It flattens things out and does not
ascend to a higher [plane]. When grief overcomes us, it tells us, "Rest
easy; suffering is just as necessary as joy," but it does not save us from
suffering. When temptation defeats us and our life threatens to collapse
into moral crisis, it preaches to us: "Be brave, [for] evil is also needed.
From an atheistic viewpoint it is just as necessary as good." It does not
set the human being's feet on the foundation of moral norms. It makes
him the prey of blind forces that corrupt his soul and his life, and it
laments, at the end, "How tragic! How beautiful!" While the questions
multiply, this worldview leaves personality without a rudder. Where
should he steer the fragile ship that is his poor life? It sings thin songs
of the wreck of his soul, of the joy of life, of his great guilt. And when
a person in those bitter difficulties lifts up his heart and seeks help
from on high, it wipes away his tears with the thought "Human, the
God you seek is the eternal harmony of contrasts; he is just as inwardly
warped as you are yourself and is only justified in the atheistic sense."

This worldview also deprives the human being of the power of moral
exertion, the power and the impulse toward self-mastery and victory
over self. It does not make a personality of the human being because
personality is synthesis—it is the victory over the contrast. This worldview sucks the life out of a person and leaves him to view himself as
a great comedian on the stage that is the world or as a poor soul who
is doomed to play a tragic role. The highest that [this worldview] can

reach is to place the human being next to life and then to show him the ridiculous or the dramatic in the whole of his existence. But in the midst of the struggle that is life itself, it leaves him weak, without a leg to stand on, wandering forward without a firm foundation.

Do you know the stirring words that Ibsen[18] has Maximus say in his great tragedy *Emperor and Galilean*?[19] Emperor Julius has died, having fallen in battle. His life has been a failure, a hopeless failure, and all the ideals for which he strove have fallen away. At this death, Maximus the magician, who had often advised the emperor and had driven him toward evil, is standing by him, and then this mysterious figure says,

> Loved, and misled him.—No, not I!
>
> Misled like Cain. Misled like Judas. Your God is a prodigal God, Galileans! He uses up many souls.
>
> Wast thou not, after all, the chosen one—thou victim of necessity?
>
> What is life worth? All is sport and make-believe.—To *will* is to *have to will*.[20]

Everything is a game. That is the sorry thought with which this world-view comes to its conclusion.

Finally, in a few words I want to sketch out theistic monism for you—or, preferably stated, Christianity. At this point, we do not want to go into this deeply, given that we will immerse ourselves in it later. But in connection with what has been said, we need to point out a few lines [of thought].

Christianity begins with the unconditional recognition of the terrible dichotomy. It places good and evil, suffering and joy, irrevocably against one another and seeks no bridge between them. Nonetheless, with all its energy, it sets up a defense against dualism. It does this, in the first place, by pointing out earnestly that evil is not eternal and is not from God,

---

18 Henrik Ibsen (1828–1906), the Norwegian playwright.—Ed.

19 Henrik Ibsen, *Emperor and Galilean: A World-Historic Drama*, ed. William Archer (New York: Scribner and Welford, 1890).—Ed.

20 Ibsen, *Emperor and Galilean*, 325.—Ed.

that it does not correspond to the material world and is not rooted in the material world. Evil is moral disruption. It is a wrong direction within the human soul. It is not a new creation. It has brought forth nothing essentially new. Rather, it is negation. It is a breaking, a disbanding [of the good]. The only true unity is in God. He is pure light, eternal light.

By stating it in this way, [Christianity] makes the human being fully responsible for evil. It does not excuse him, does not say that he could have done differently because he is composed of heterogeneous elements. It relentlessly demands of him good, love, knowledge, virtue, blessedness. The dichotomy that is in the human being is indeed present, but it should be absent. In every regard, it should be condemned. The human being must give himself to the good with all his heart and all his might.

When he does this, no piece of his life is cut off. He does not have to turn away from the sensible world toward isolation because sin is not hidden in the world or in isolation. It is present wherever the [human] heart is [found]. But when the heart has been made clean, a person may enter into the fullness of life, into the fullness of the world, in spirit and in matter. Then everything is open to him because soul and body, matter and spirit, are both glorious creations of the one great Maker. When the human being does [what is] good, no part of his life is cut off. Rather, it is only the bent direction of his life that is set straight. He is morally reborn. At that same moment, he can serve God in both soul and body and can help his neighbor.

This is why Christianity maintains the ideal of personality with unshakable firmness. It may well be that a person is confused in the dichotomy, but the human being is and remains destined for unity. That synthesis is his glorious vocation. Good and evil do not stand opposite one another as two substances, as two halves that have equal rights. They are two directions that pull the human being apart. It is only when he seeks God with his whole heart that he finds this unity. God wants to call every human being to personality. Every person must become [a personality] so that he may bear the image of God, may reflect the glory of God—and God is unity.

Therefore, Christianity gives the human being a sense of guilt. It deprives him of any excuse. But when it humbles him by making him fully responsible, it also simultaneously extends to him an incalculably valuable privilege: that he may have a firm foundation in his life. It gives him direction and steers him. It gives him an ideal, the power of moral exertion. It propels him into life as an unceasing battle against himself, against the powers of evil in his own heart. It gives him a norm, a commandment, energy.

When he finds himself broken by despair, it does not comfort him with "You could have done nothing about it; it is all a game!" Rather, it makes him bow down under the guilt of his own broken life and carries him back to his Father's house. From far off, it points him to the land of unity, which no sin or despair may enter. To become a personality is your vocation; put to death, then, the powers of sin that corrupt your life!

One day, [your life] will become a unity. Through the path of the new birth and conversion, the soul approaches the gates of the kingdom of unity. Far off in the distance, it shows us the blurred outline of the new kingdom. It says, "Oh human, strive at every stage of your life. Your soul has been torn apart, your life left desolate. Grasp the saving, forgiving grace of the eternal Father, and go forward in his power, leaning on him, on the path to your calling, toward your ideal."

This worldview pulls the human being upward. It does not deny [that] the dichotomy [is there], but it does deny the dichotomy's right [to be there].

Evil cannot be justified. We must not accept it. This worldview is able to make the human being into a personality in that rich and deep sense of unity, of synthesis. With all his powers and gifts, with wondrous inner harmony, the reborn person enters the kingdom of God.

Passive Knowing

IT IS NOT POSSIBLE for us to deal with all the different worldviews broadly and more or less comprehensively. The overabundance of material would quickly cause us to lose our focus. For the goal that we have in mind, such a comprehensive overview is also unnecessary. It will suffice for us to consider a few types of systems that have been greatly influential. Because of this, we will limit ourselves to more recent Western philosophy.

In many regards, Western thinking is easily distinguished from its Eastern [equivalents]. The Westerner is an entirely different sort of person from the peoples of Asia. The Eastern person attaches great worth to his inner life. The more sober-minded Westerner's view is more outwardly focused. He believes in the world, in matter, and knows [*kent*] the strong impulse to exploit the world according to his own needs. He considers life as reality, as urgent, and is in little danger of losing himself in idle dreams. The Easterner retains the deep intuition that this world remains untrue, that it is a veil over the only true being. He believes in the spirit as the only reality and thus looks down on all worldly works and desires. To the contrary, the Westerner feels at home in the world, creates as good an existence for himself as possible, and expects the sources of help necessary to him from nature. One could say, Western culture is more technically oriented, and Eastern culture is more mystically oriented; Western culture is more realistic,

Eastern more idealistic. Naturally, one must be careful with such general sketches. Whoever would deny all [traces of] mysticism in the West would be just as wrong as the person who views Easterners exclusively as otherworldly zealots. Thankfully, the contrasts are not so stark. It is more a difference in accent, especially expressed in how the West has also produced idealists and mystics, although in the West such figures have always remained lone individuals. They have never been able to bring entire peoples under their sway.

It is normal to begin describing the history of more recent Western philosophy with that great and capacious cultural shift commonly known as the Renaissance. The Renaissance brought about major changes, set Western thought in very new directions, and should indeed be considered an extremely significant event.

Now it is obvious that within the limits of our investigation, the different factors and elements of that shift cannot be dealt with extensively. We must make do with a very limited, general characterization so that we can move over immediately to the great spiritual movements that have come about because of it. If we want to form some kind of clear concept of the Renaissance, we might be best served by comparing medieval art with that of the fourteenth to the sixteenth centuries.

Medieval art was predominantly symbolic and closed. Architecture ruled over all other artistic expressions, and in that architecture, the ascending line dominated as a symbolic pointer to the [exhortation] "Lift up your hearts!" An altar, a small relic chest, in short, everything, was conceived of as an edifice, with pointed arches and other architectural figures. Sculpture did indeed develop, but the figures were placed in niches and into frames, and as such, they accepted the forms commanded by their places in the building. In general, they were tall, too slender, and the symbolic was also predominant in the representation of their physiques. The posture of the hands, the facial expression, the folds in the clothing, were not natural, not real, but rather symbolic. They were entirely suited to the idea [that undergirded] the whole setup of the building. Portraiture painted its figures with golden backgrounds, was sober in whatever else it included, and was averse to being concrete.

It did not bring forth people of flesh and blood. The colors of their robes, especially dark red and blue, were symbolic and had a deeper meaning. In all this, we must not think that these phenomena should be viewed as technical inadequacies but rather that they were strongly grounded in the artists' intentions. They must be seen as expressions of culture, equally as sketches of the ways of thinking and feeling of people in those days.

Contrast this with the art of the Renaissance. You immediately sense the great distinction. The images move out of their niches and arches and become independent figures. They take on flesh and blood; their relationships become looser, freer, more natural. They are also set free from their architectural milieu and no longer have the forms and lines that that building's milieu gave them. Sculpture was developed into its own art form and no longer had to serve as an accompaniment to architecture. The same is also true of portraiture. There we also see the figures become more natural. Here and there, for example, we begin to see a painting that portrays a Madonna on a grassy field with flowers. Faces take on expression, you begin to find personalities within them, human beings with faults and ideals. The symbolic withdraws more and more into the background, and an irrepressible love for nature—for reality in all its diversity—bursts forth victoriously from every side.

These simple differences cannot be appreciated enough. They typify a revolution on spiritual terrain that then spreads out everywhere else. And this revolution can be more closely characterized at different points. Medieval culture was an exceptionally uniform [*einheitliche*] culture. In science, everything was subjected to theology, and theology ruled over all the other sciences. In art, everything was subjected to architecture, and this architecture itself served as a symbolic pointer toward the great spiritual realities. Even the way society [itself] was built up bore a unified character. Ultimately, it was the spiritual government, the pope, who exercised rule over worldly powers. The entirety of life, the whole of thinking, was understood in [the idea of] unity. Everything belonged together. There was an idea that penetrated everything. Now this is precisely what changed in the Renaissance. In art, sculpture and portraiture wrestled themselves free of architecture. They became distinct terrains with their own ideas and intentions. The sciences more or less freed themselves from theology, sought their own methods, their own paths, their own sources. On its own, this does not contain a struggle, a contrast, although the possibility—the likelihood, even—of contrast began to increase. In society, ultimately, worldly and spiritual powers increasingly occupied separate spheres, distinct domains. Life itself became more varied and specialized. This is one of the most essential traits of the great spiritual revolution of those days: the dividing of life [into different] areas. The [old] architectural unity was broken. Difference proved victorious.

A second, and no less weighty, trait was love for nature. Medieval culture lived from the inside outward. All expressions were symbolic, pointers toward spiritual realities. The man of the Renaissance lived more from the outside inward. He saw, noticed, devoted himself wholeheartedly to nature, discovered beautiful treasures beyond himself. That was a kind of reaction in him. He began to study nature, and in astronomy and physics [he] discovered rules that people had not previously supposed. He found it glorious to look on nature, to be amazed at it. And in his artistic expressions, he was always oriented toward the ever-changing and always beautiful model—nature itself—that he knew around himself. In the Middle Ages, nature was always seen as something more or less sinful, as something that distracts from mystical life, from interaction with God. They thought of separation from the world, withdrawing into a monastery, as the ideal. In nature, the modern person discovered a treasury that overwhelmed him, and precisely in that world, which surrounded him, he found the greatness of God.

We can see a third trait here: the Renaissance aimed for personality. It took pleasure in sketching the human being in his idiosyncrasies, in his character. In considering human beings, medieval culture focused only on his relationship to God and saw only that ascending line in his life. The Renaissance also saw his relationship to life, to the world. It saw multiple lines. It discovered diversity.

This greater exposure for personality had serious consequences. In religious intuitions, it meant that a stronger accent was also laid on the subject. That was one of the factors in the great movement of the Reformation, which proceeded from Luther[1] in Germany and also arose in other countries. "Over against the objective materializing of the benefits of salvation, the Reformers laid the stress on the religious subject."[2]

When you consider all these different symptoms, you have a certain impression of the significance of this cultural shift. It is indeed a Renaissance, a new birth. Taken alone in this way, this movement is only characterized; it is not explained as such. In fact, such mighty shifts are not easily given to [facile] explanations. We can gather all sorts of material to make clear how it developed, but there always remains mystery in this. History itself is full of mighty puzzles. What is crystal clear, however, is that this movement revealed itself first and most strongly in Italy. There all the elements necessary to the emergence of such a new idea were present. There was also a certain economic well-being that is not the cause of [the Renaissance] but that is a condition of new cultural development. From Italy, the movement quickly spread out to all Europe, calling new thoughts and ideas to life everywhere. Now this is the movement that we must watch carefully if we want to give our account of the development of science and philosophy in the modern age. It also stimulated the empiricist movement in philosophy that sprang up particularly in England.

That empiricism is permeated by one idea, namely, that we are dependent on our sensations for the acquisition of knowledge. We are passive, above all, on the path to knowing. We must let things speak, and we ourselves must be silent. Summarized briefly, that is the empiricist confession of faith. As we have already noted, that empiricism grew up and developed particularly in English soil, during and after the reign of Queen Elizabeth[3]—that is, from the second half of the sixteenth century.

1   Martin Luther (1483–1546), the German Protestant Reformer.—Ed.
2   Herman Bavinck, *Philosophy of Revelation: A New Annotated Edition*, ed. Cory Brock and Nathaniel Gray Sutanto (Peabody, MA: Hendrickson, 2018), 4.—Ed.
3   Queen Elizabeth I (1533–1603), queen of England and Ireland from 1558 to 1603.—Ed.

Francis Bacon[4] is usually described as the founder of this empiricism. Naturally, we must be careful with such a claim. As a method, as an intuition, empiricism was present long before Bacon set it out in a philosophical manner. In a certain sense, the great thinkers were the creators of the history of philosophy, although not as though they suddenly moved in entirely new directions. They were much more those who brought all sorts of tendencies, which lie slumbering everywhere, to consciousness, to clarity, to life.

Taken as such, empiricism was doubtless one of the offshoots of the Renaissance. In the Middle Ages, especially in its last period, science was practiced from the works of Aristotle,[5] to whom a certain authority was given. All sorts of ideas were borrowed from him, and these ideas were then differently combined, although in essence one rarely departed from him. Through deduction, by proceeding from a few common foundational truths, one tried to see and to order science in its entirety. In principle, the Renaissance broke with this method. It wanted to perceive freely, had a powerful need to discover new things by itself, and did not bow the knee before Aristotle's authority. In different areas, especially in astronomy, this newly awakened science had already shown that Aristotle should not be considered infallible. The great discovery that the earth moves around the sun and not the sun around the earth is one of the consequences of freeing oneself from the grip of that mighty ancient thinker.

From that moment on, the necessity of following different methods was felt. One could not deduce all the further particulars from a few simple presuppositions. [Rather,] a person had to perceive for himself and take up [what was perceived] into himself. That need arose among the Italian natural philosophers but was made into a system in English empiricism. To quite some degree, the only path to certain knowledge is perception, the empirical, passively letting [things] work themselves into you.

4 Francis Bacon (1561–1626), the English philosopher and statesman. In the original, Bavinck incorrectly lists the year of Bacon's death as 1627.—Ed.
5 Aristotle (384–322 BC), an ancient Greek philosopher and formerly a student of Plato.—Ed.

All this was expressed clearly and with emphasis by Bacon. We must begin by quietly perceiving. It is all about conquering new knowledge, discovering new things. In that time, there was hunger for new experiences, new ideas. The old was thought to be insufficient, and above all, new concepts were sought out. How can we expand our science? Bacon tried to give an answer to that question.

He proposed that every seeker of science must begin by viewing the world impartially. He must not step into reality with all manner of previously established ideas because such ideas are confusing and misleading. They hinder quiet, passive perception. One must begin by knowing nothing. In everything, one must orient oneself to the object, describing, explaining what nature says to us, without constantly getting carried away with what one wishes to see. This means one must set to work inductively, beginning gently from below and building upward to the heights. One should not draw conclusions from defined ideas that one believes as certain truths but rather must stand beneath [reality] and receive. Therefore, one must also be careful about proceeding from the authority of others. The fact that Aristotle or some other great thinker has said something is in no sense a proof that it is true. One moves happily past all those authorities and says, "I want to view reality independently and quietly."

One must also be careful with one's own predisposition, with one's own most intimate convictions. They might be very nice, and sometimes useful, but one cannot let them play a part in science. It could be that reality is wholly different from what you had expected in your deepest predisposition and inclinations. In that case, you must be bold enough to venture toward that reality and sacrifice your most intimate faith. Science is self-denial. The further you move into that self-denial, the less preconceived faith you bring into [your] science, and the more easily you become a man of science.

We act as though we are actually the first people to start to think in the history of the world. What former generations have said is indeed important, but we would rather begin anew. In this, above all, we use perception of what happens in nature and sometimes also experimentation. When we do this, we begin by knowing nothing; we want to come to know everything, and so we only listen. That is the path to real science. For Bacon, it is not about science for science's sake. He sensed too keenly that science is also accompanied by practical results. The more we get to know nature, the more we gain mastery over it and can dominate it. The one leads to the other and implies the other. That he was not mistaken here can be most clearly demonstrated through the subsequent development of the natural sciences, hand in hand with technology.

It is noticeable that Bacon calls the idea of telos[6] one of the ideas that must be set aside if you want to study nature objectively. We are inclined to think that everything in the world around us is organized toward a goal, that there is a plan, a goal, hidden within it. Now [for Bacon,] that is nothing other than a preconceived assumption from which we must free ourselves if we want to take up into ourselves reality in an objective way. We might well wish that it was so [i.e., that the world was organized teleologically], but we may not proclaim this in advance. Rather, nature teaches us of indestructible, unbroken causality. It speaks to us of its conformity to laws rather than to goals. It speaks to us of necessity. We must give ourselves over to that truth peacefully and fully and must not muddle our own experiences with our own insights.

Although in many regards Bacon can be seen as the one who laid the ground for empiricism, he was not as one-sided as one might assume. He sensed full well that while science must be based on perception, it could not be equated to the sum total of perceptions. In his own way, he expressed it like this: in our science, we must not be like the ants, which simply gather their material in great heaps.[7] In this way, there are scientific people who engage in much perception but bring no line,

---

6   Original Dutch, *doelmatigheid*: teleology, the notion that the cosmos exists toward a particular goal (telos).—Ed.

7   Here Bavinck refers to Bacon's comparison of empiricists to ants, who "only collect and use" facts. See Perez Zagorin, *Francis Bacon* (Princeton, NJ: Princeton University Press, 1998), 100.—Ed.

no system, into it. We may also not resemble the spider whose whole web comes from within himself.[8] The ideal, rather, is that we discover and pursue all sorts of facts through perception but that we also work quietly on that material. That is how bees work. They gather their material everywhere but also work on it.[9] Bacon developed the ideal of all science in this way.

When we take a moment to view these ideas more closely, it seems like we are only dealing with a way of working, with a couple of logical observations on scientific method. In reality, however, much more lurks behind it, and many more and larger things flow forth from these bare ideas. We immediately start to see this when we ask ourselves which worldview was preached by Bacon and his followers. Then it emerges that they taught us of a world that is dominated in every part by an almighty law of causation. There is one truth that is foundational to all science: causality. Everything happens according to the law of cause and effect. In every domain of our knowing [*weten*], we will be able to find that principle. From here on, this causality is conceptualized in a strongly mechanical sense. It turns everything into a great machine in which every occurrence is absolutely determined by the occurrence that came before it. This emerged clearly with Bacon but was more clearly pronounced by some of his followers, among them, Thomas Hobbes.[10] This concept of mechanical causality was unusually attractive to the thought of that period. The great astronomers had shown that in their revolutions and paths, the celestial bodies obey fixed natural laws. And now the idea arose that in the same way, every other thing could be explained in its movements and directions. If that were true, what conquests lay in wait! In a short space of time, one could master every scientific terrain and break open each secret with the golden key that was the concept of causality. The world had no more mysteries. Everything was necessity. The only thing that remained to be done

---

8   Zagorin, *Francis Bacon*, 100.—Ed.

9   Zagorin, *Francis Bacon*, 100.—Ed.

10 Thomas Hobbes (1588–1679), an English philosopher best known for his book *Leviathan*.—Ed.

was to pursue the forms of causality, the ways in which it is active in different areas.

To spend a moment following what is suggested in this idea is appropriate. Here we are dealing with a striking example of the imperialism of a scientific concept. A certain concept (that of mechanical causality), first borrowed from astronomy and mechanics, suddenly arises as the scientific concept *par excellence* and is called on in other areas [of reality] to explain all other phenomena. That is a suggestion; it is a hypothesis. The idea triumphantly [proclaims] that the world is so extremely simply constructed that with a single concept, everything can be explained, that all phenomena can readily be recorded through a single way of looking [at them].

However far one dares to take this, it seems that some even thought it was possible to explain the soul in this way. The soul is also a machine. The one idea gives rise to the other; one representation [*voorstelling*] calls for another. The soul is ruled by firm laws (known as laws of association),[11] which fully explain each psychical phenomenon. The one follows from the other: once you have sufficient insight into the whole mechanism, you can determine each human deed with absolute purity, just as you can predict the going down of the sun. The world is made of two groups of realities: material and mental. We get to know the first through sensory perception and the second through self-consideration and reflection. In both hemispheres, however, causality rules. Both are like gigantic machines in which each cog locks into another and each movement can be calculated. This is the idea that is taught in different [forms] by empiricism through its representatives. Alongside this, it is taught that this concept should not be seen as a preconceived idea but as the fruit of experience. Perception teaches us that it is so. Perception lets us see causality everywhere and [shows us] that we should give ourselves over to it.

---

11   Here Bavinck refers to the laws of association—contiguity, repetition, attention, pleasure-pain, and similarity—formulated by Aristotle and later revived in the seventeenth century by John Locke (1632–1704), an English philosopher commonly known as the "father of liberalism."—Ed.

We might wish that it were not so, but we must submit to the way things actually are. In summary, there is one way to knowledge [*kennis*], which is perception and the conclusion built on it. And there is also one explanatory principle for all phenomena in every area: mechanical causality.

If you thought for a moment that these views corresponded to reality, what would the consequence be for the life of the personality?

In the first place, this: human freedom, activity, spontaneity would cease to exist. The human being is a machine, a tiny component in a huge world-machine. He is made to react by mighty cosmic laws, which nothing can escape. He is a purely passive being. He is led, carried along as though by a stream that he can never swim against—[a stream] that simply carries him along.

If this were true, all morality, with all the responsibility that accompanies it, would immediately be done for. There are no norms, and neither can norms exist because there is only one law, the law of nature, that holds everything tightly in its grip.

As well as this, how could we know those laws? There are two paths to knowledge—perception and reflection. Does sensory perception teach us of the existence of norms? No, it teaches us only of causality. Does reflection teach us of the existence of norms? No, at most, it teaches us that many people walk through life under the illusion that there are norms. The laws of nature also rule in the psychical.

Furthermore, is there a God? It is not impossible. But if he does exist, he is impossible for us to know. There are, after all, only two paths to knowledge. Does sensory perception teach us of the existence of God? No. The same is also true of reflection. Therefore, it is indeed true that God might exist, but he nonetheless remains endlessly far from us. He withdraws into the unrecognizable distance. We have no [suitable] organs with which to approach him. We can climb up toward him with all sorts of conclusions, but those conclusions are already of very little worth. God becomes a lesser worthy reality, a reality of the second order. We can take it into account, but beyond this, it is of little importance to us. He lies beyond the realm of knowability. This is the idea that we call deism. God stands far beyond the creation, and we can consider the world as an entity unto itself.

And finally, does teleology exist? We are inclined to think it does. But do we have any grounds for this? Nature teaches us only causality. Whether there is a goal, a sense, a meaning, in our lives, cannot be said with certainty [because] it falls beyond the realm of knowability.

As such, in practice, a number of the great values [that we attach] to life are denied. A number of the great puzzles of [life and] the world are also reasoned away—the puzzle of the will, of activity, of the sense of guilt, of morality. And all that [is so] in the name of experience, of the empirical. The empirical teaches us inexorable causality and knows nothing of freedom, of spontaneity. Seen psychologically, this direction means a noticeable overgrowth of the [soul's] passive functions. Human life is resolved in passivity. [The human being] is passive in his knowing [*kennen*] because knowing equals perceiving, receiving. He is passive in his willing, because willing equals being driven by mighty laws of nature. That which is passive is the only reality. With this, [his] psychical balance is shattered in a remarkable way. The active functions of thinking, willing, and becoming are either pushed to the side or misunderstood in every sense of their meaning. Empiricism sketches out for us a personality from which different central functions have been excised from [their] operative [roles] and thus that is completely dead. In its personality, it takes on a beautiful unity—[indeed, its] unity even comes to the fore. But that unity is won at the cost of different vital powers, by simply denying the [soul's] active functions. Through this, the [soul's] balance immediately slides to one side. Suppose that such a worldview begins to dominate; it then pulls the personality apart and then makes the personality limp and lifeless, its powers reduced to a rubber ball. The most awful part of this, however, is that it places excuses directly into that person's lifeless hands: "I am just a small cog in a great world-machine! I am completely passive! And God? God is so far away, so infinitely far off!"

From the very moment that this worldview started to emerge, that process of disintegration also began. In the long run, it would lead to [the personality] falling apart. It is too simplistic; it denies the existence of muscles and knows only nerves. In England, from that time onward, another movement ran parallel to this empiricist, deistic one that was more mystically oriented. It found its bulwark at Cambridge University and its great representatives in men like Moore[12] and Cudworth.[13] This mystical movement was more oriented toward Neoplatonism and fought against superficial empiricism with great vigor.

More important is that, because of its one-sidedness, empiricism steadily began destroying itself. [Its advocates] got into difficulty on the issue of morality. It is indeed easy to set all morality to the side with a swish of the hand, but life is not well served by this. Life needs moral laws, but where will we get them? A series of great thinkers has dared to construct a new morality. That is no easy task for someone who stands on empiricist ground because we can never perceive norms. And yet people strive for this and give all sorts of descriptions of virtue. In practical terms, [those who have done so] never rose above the quite superficial and fairly meaningless thought that the good is that which leads to "the greatest happiness [for] the greatest number" (Priestley).[14] Someone may indeed be an empiricist and maintain the absolute passivity of human life, but in fact he does not dare follow the consequences of that [absolute passivity]. And in that [unwillingness to be consistent], that person does himself credit!

More important still is the fact that empiricism is the cause of its own breakdown. It devours itself. To understand this, we must move into deeper waters and occupy ourselves with the philosophical thoughts of John Locke and David Hume.[15] We have Locke to thank for a detailed and capacious analysis of our knowing [*weten*]. He proceeds from [the claim that] perception and reflection are the channels through which our knowledge [*kennis*] flows. The intellect, though, proceeds from

---

12 George Edward Moore (1873–1958), an English philosopher and professor of philosophy at the University of Cambridge.—Ed.
13 Ralph Cudworth (1617–1688), an English philosopher and leading exponent of Cambridge Platonism.—Ed.
14 Joseph Priestley (1733–1804), an English polymath.—Ed.
15 David Hume (1711–1776), a Scottish philosopher who wielded great influence in the fields of empiricism, naturalism, and skepticism.—Ed.

the material that is acquired in these ways to work through it and thus tries to pierce through the phenomena. It succeeds at this, but however much further the intellect removes itself from perception, its results become all the more uncertain. This, then, is why we never agree with each other when we reason about God, immortality, and so forth. We are dealing with things of great magnitude that the intellect cannot actually handle, and we must therefore end up going astray. For this reason, it is so necessary that we always ask ourselves carefully, "What does perception teach me, and what do I add to it with my intellect?"

Whenever we move along that path, we quickly come to surprising results. At this very moment, what do you perceive? You will say, "A brown, round table." Closer analysis reveals that not to be true. You do see a brown circle. If you touch it, you feel something hard. From the play of the light, you can also see that it is smooth. That is all correct. But you do not see a table. A table is a thing, something independent, a substance. What you perceive are attributes: the color (brown), the hardness, the smoothness, and so on. None of that, though, is a table.

Yes, you say, but those attributes do not simply hang in the air. If I see brown, there must be something that is brown. Those attributes cannot exist in isolation. There must be a thing, a substance that bears them, to which those qualities can be attributed. An attribute is unthinkable without its bearer. In other words, our perception teaches us of an innumerable number of attributes. I see brown and blue, I hear sounds, I feel hard and soft [materials], and so on. Behind all those attributes, I always think of substances—chests, tables, chairs that are hard, brown, and so forth. I can never perceive the substances themselves; I do not have a sense for that. The only things that I can perceive are attributes. I note in passing that we are going to see these things entirely differently [later]. Eventually, the concept of substance itself was completely changed, but we cannot go into that at this point. I direct those who are interested, for example, to Prof. Dr. J. Clay's concise work *The Development of Thinking*.[16]

16 Jacob Clay, *De ontwikkeling van het denken: een inleiding in de problemen der kennisleer* (Arnhem: Van Loghum, Slaterus, and Visser, 1920). Clay (1882–1955) was a Dutch polymath who, like J. H. Bavinck, spent time in Indonesia. See Klaas van Berkel, Albert

There was something astonishing in Locke's discovery. Think about this clearly: Locke argued that we cannot perceive the material world. We only perceive attributes, but our intellect thinks the substances themselves lie behind them because we cannot conceive of those attributes without their bearers. Locke clarified this thought with a well-known example: an Indian philosopher learned that the world was borne up by an elephant, and the elephant by a giant tortoise. When someone then asked, "By what is the tortoise then borne up?" he answered, "By something different, but what, I do not know." It is the same[, he argued,] for us. What we perceive are attributes. But what do those attributes rest on? On the substance that bears them. But what then is that substance? We do not know [*weten*] what.

The whole of this conclusion is thus of such great importance because it actually overthrows empiricism. One of these [must be true]: either [we believe in empiricism, or] we keep on believing in the existence of things, of substances, of a material world. But then we must immediately recognize, along with this, that we do not know only by perceiving but rather that with our intellect, our thinking, we posit, as it were, the very thing that matters. If we do not want to follow this path, we [must] fall into skepticism. Does the world indeed exist? Do things exist? Is everything an illusion?

This resounds even more strongly when we also take into account the fact that many of the attributes that we perceive are themselves also quite subjective. The color, for example, that we attribute to things is subjective. A color-blind person sees them differently. Our eyes are so equipped that they perceive colors in such a way, but [what they perceive] could quite conceivably be completely different. All taken together, what we know [*weten*] through perception is but a poor morsel. The most important, the thing that really matters, is what we add with our intellect. We perceive attributes and not "things," and whether these attributes are as we perceive them

van Helden, and Lodewijk Palm, *A History of Science in the Netherlands: Survey, Themes, and Reference* (Leiden: Brill, 1999), 435–36.—Ed.

[to be] is also uncertain. From this, we see the paltry results of the analysis of perception.

Locke's important investigation was further advanced by the no less perceptive thinker David Hume. In various regards, Hume far exceeded his predecessor, namely, in that while Locke had subjected the concept of substance to earnest criticism, Hume focused more particularly on the concept of causality. We can state it like this: Hume did the same thing to the concept of causality that Locke did to the concept of substance.

Before all else, this means that Hume began to analyze the idea of causality more closely. Imagine that I place a kettle of water on a fire. At some point, the water will boil, the lid will begin to pop up and down, steam will escape, and I will hear that distinctive whistle from the boiling water—all sorts of phenomena, thus, that follow one another. Do they also follow *from* each other? May I say that the fire is the cause of the water boiling and that the boiling is the cause of the lid moving, and so on? We do believe this. But can we perceive it? Hume says no!

I throw a ball against a wall. The ball springs back according to the law that the angle of incidence is equal to the angle of reflection. Must that happen in this way? Are we dealing here with causality? With necessity? We can say that it always happens, that we cannot imagine it otherwise, that the one always happens as does the other, but what we can never perceive is precisely that it *must* happen. We only see that certain phenomena always and constantly proceed in the same order, that if the one happens, the other will always happen. But that is always only a temporary sequence. Our perception can never, ever show us that it also must happen in this way, that a necessary causality exists between the phenomena. Our perception never goes beyond observing that certain phenomena perpetually proceed in the same sequence.

But to what, then, do we owe the concept of causality? It seems we ourselves contribute it. Perception does not teach it to us, but rather we add it to [our] perceptions. Hume thought this phenomenon was best accounted for by pointing to a certain law of association, the law of contiguity. In that context, he understood this phenomenon, that when the soul has perceived two phenomena, *a* and *b*, in connection with each other a few times, it is then immediately reminded of *b* whenever it sees *a*. When *a* appears, it expects that *b* will then also appear. To the soul, these two have now become so closely bound that it cannot imagine that one does not naturally bring the other along with it. When this expectation is confirmed time and time again, the soul begins to trust that whenever *a* has been, *b* also *must* come. In other words, it begins to summarize a habit that exists within itself as a law that is operative out there in the world. It begins to speak of causality; it begins to recount that the one causes the other. In all this, however, it takes a leap that is not actually permitted. And what is worse, it continues to give the appearance of perceiving this causality, as though empiricism has taught it that causality exists. That is a great illusion because perception can only ever teach an always recurring sequence. If *a* happens, *b* also happens. That it also has to be so, that it could not be any different, that *a* causes *b*, all goes far beyond perception itself.

We can casually note, at this point, that we face all these phenomena very differently from Hume. In the first place, the concept of causality has undergone notable development, and our thoughts on it have changed very much. Nor do we attach the same meaning to the laws of association on which Hume based his argument. Hume set out the matters in question far too simplistically, which was later shown most clearly by Kant.

But [we note this only] casually! The fact is that Hume's investigations were of very great importance. After all, what is the issue here? If what Hume says is true, every consistent empiricist must actually bring the existence of causality more or less into doubt. Above all, empiricism proceeds on the basis that we owe our knowledge to perception. The intellect works on those perceptions and draws conclusions from them, but those conclusions are less certain in any case. [With empiricism] we have no such firm ground beneath our feet. Rather, [under our feet] there is room for all manner of subjective convictions. If the concept of causality is a concept that we do not owe to perception but that we ourselves install, then we must also consider the concept of causality as a second-order concept, as a certainty of a lower order. With this, though, the whole of empiricism falls down. It is the sensory impressions that cause perceptions within us; our perceptions are worked on by impulses from outside ourselves, which work themselves into our senses. A causal relationship exists between the impulse and the perception. When the concept of causality becomes uncertain in this way, all our perceptions simultaneously become uncertain. The one falls with the other. And with this, all empiricism comes to an end.

History thus places before us the remarkable phenomenon that empiricism devoured itself. [Human] thought overtook the great one-sidedness that had gone wrong from the beginning, and new light came to shine on the great questions that people saw before them. That beautiful image of the world [*wereldbeeld*] in which causality summarized and governed everything, that seemed to rest on the empirical, and that robed itself in the battle cry of "perception" ultimately seemed to hold within itself very many subjective things. The great concepts to which it pointed, substance and causality, are not concepts that we can know through perception. We subordinate them to perceptions, but they themselves rest on the conclusions of the intellect.

These realizations meant the end of empiricism. It is always worth retaining a clear view of these things. [In the present day,] the worldview of many an untrained thinker demonstrates a striking similarity to the worldview of seventeenth-century empiricism. How many people there are who say with enviable decisiveness: "I only believe in what I can see!" If only all these were able to analyze what they say. If only they could be brought up to speed on empiricism! That simple little word, *perception*, contains so much. Perception is not exclusively passively letting things outside us speak to us. We perceive thinkingly. In our perceiving, we enrich, apply, distort the content of our perceptions without us even being aware [of doing so]. That is all much more complicated than some may think from afar.

Empiricism is a contortion of the personality. It lays all the emphasis on the passive functions, and it does not perceive that in our passive deeds, we are also active and creative. This was gradually discovered through careful analysis. In the course of history, English empiricism—which had as a distinctive trait that it clung to the idea of mechanical causality, in which it sought the key to unlock all the secrets [of the cosmos]—came to the conclusion that this entire presupposition was nothing other than an intuition. It was a worldvision, not a worldview. It was not robed in perception, however much it called on it. In its deepest essence, it was a grasping of the human mind that allowed itself to be mesmerized by one overwhelming idea.

All this will become more deeply valuable to you when you focus again on the personality. English empiricism taught absolute passivity. We are passive in our knowing, and actually, we can only perceive because when we start thinking, we confuse ourselves at every moment. We are also passive in our life. We are dragged and pushed along by mighty laws of nature that bring us where they wish. We ourselves are machines, small fragments of the great world-machine. But if that is true, we have also explained our poverty and moral misery. We cannot help falling into evil so often or not doing what we know we must. In one fell swoop, we have reasoned away our existential crisis. We have no more guilt or responsibility. The soul sees itself as the victim, the driftwood tossed back and forth on the waves of the laws of nature. All norms are broken into pieces, and we have justified our poverty.

On this point, this intuition contains something attractive. It takes the tension away from us. It comforts us with regard to evil: "I am only passive. I can do nothing about it if things go wrong for me. I was duped by powers against which I can do nothing." The soul creeps, as it were, toward this intuition to rid itself of the tension of guilt, of responsibility, of freedom. For this reason, this worldvision roots itself so deeply in the human being. If I may say it so bluntly, the human being has a vested interest in thinking like this because if he lets himself think so, he stamps into pieces his own life's goal, his ideals, his freedom, but then he also escapes the grip of his sense of poverty and guilt. This is why this intuition—the intuition of absolute passivity—continually returns in the human being, through the entire line of knowing and living.

And of course, this intuition is not entirely unjust. Passivity is one side of our existence—and a very important side [at that]. In part, we are passive in our knowing. We are directed by impressions from outside ourselves. We are also passive in our living. Often our willing is not free, since it is co-opted by powerful necessity. Perhaps we ourselves are more passive than we assume. Passivity is a side of our existence, and we do well to recognize it.

And yet it is not the only side. You can look differently at living and knowing. There is activity in our knowing, in our thinking, in our perceiving. There is also activity in our living. There is freedom, norm, responsibility. There is a God and a mighty plan for the world in which everything is ordered. There is an ideal—a goal and a destination for life. There is also guilt. There is sin. You can see life as a hand that you have been dealt; you can also see it as a deed. It happens to you, and you also happen to it. The wondrous dichotomy of activity and passivity lies riveted together—so closely that we cannot see the joint—deep in our soul. We cannot closely make out where one stops and the other begins.

This is why the worldvision that is empiricism must fall apart. Personality itself must react against it, because [the personality], with all its riches, could find no peace in that intuition. [Empiricism] could enchant minds for a moment, but the direction of its suggestions had to be rejected. Personality itself broke the chains that empiricism had laid on it.

Yes, and more strongly still, [human] thinking itself overtook it. This worldvision could not grow up into a worldview, because when it went looking for grounds and motives, its weapons fell from its hands. Thinking itself laid bare its problems.

Even in the most passive functions of your soul, in your concepts of matter and of causality, you are powerfully spontaneous; you prove the majesty of your mind, which climbs upward beyond perception and works thinkingly on that perception. The two great concepts, substance and causality, do not simply fall into your lap. In a certain sense, you must create them with your intellect, even though perception continually gives you impulses and direction. Faith in the soul's own activity sounds the death knell for empiricism. The soul is indeed small, is indeed receptive, is indeed passive. It is often a slave, but it is also free and powerful and rich and large and regal. The history of the soul [*zielsgeschiedenis*] plays a small part in our view of the history of human thought, but that small part has value for us all.

The concept of mechanical causality is a formidable one. It made Western science great. But it is not and cannot ever become the key to all mysteries, or the philosopher's stone. It cannot precisely because this concept is a creation of the soul. [Indeed,] it was the activity of the intellect that gave birth to this concept.

The Power of Reason

WE CAN BARELY IMAGINE the great shift in mentality in Western Europe that was triggered by the Renaissance. That movement's immediate consequences were entirely new orientations [of thought and life]. It was a thoroughgoing revolution in thinking and feeling.

After all, [before the Renaissance] scholasticism had maintained a fairly simple posture toward all sorts of problems. In every question, it could call on one authority or another and was founded on a mix of general truths recognized by all. The teaching of the church gave firmness and peace to all thinking. If there were disagreements, people in any case had a shared starting point and made recourse to the same doctrines. The teaching of the church was a great and extensively worked-out system from which conclusions could be drawn in every area. To call on a church father, on a council, on the authority of some great theologian, on Aristotle (who enjoyed a distinct authority on philosophical questions), was to make a powerful argument. With all differences in ideas that came to expression in the Middle Ages, people nonetheless had a common, firm foundation in a great mass of basic premises—[premises] that they did not readily call into dispute.

This distinctive posture also had a considerable influence on the method of scientific research [in that era]. That method was preferably deductive, descending from the great to the small, from the more to the fewer. People were univocal on the issues of greater importance.

Here people were univocal on the essence of God, they were certain regarding the creation of the human being, and from that they could descend to the smaller issues. "If this is true, then that must also be true." In this way, one could approach each different question from the great foundational questions, and because one felt certain about the foundational issues, one also stood on solid ground in the smaller issues. In fact, it was an issue of sharp distinctions, of seeing clearly which consequences proceeded from particular ideas, of combining well. Who was master of this easily surpassed his opponents. In a plausible way, he could deduce conclusions about practical life from the great basic premises (which everyone accepted). This was the way philosophical thinking developed in the later Middle Ages.

Now the Renaissance brought an indescribable revolution to this posture. It cut off what had always been lifted up beyond the realms of doubt. It attacked precisely those basic premises, rejected the authority of the church fathers and councils, scoffed at Aristotle's authority, and ended up posing completely different questions [from those of the medievals]. In a certain sense, nothing was left firm; everything was doubted, subject to reason; all foundational ideas were weighed up anew. A new freedom of thinking was awakened, which wanted to free itself completely from all authority and forge new paths independently. That meant that on all terrain, the questions of morality, political science, physics, and psychology, of philosophy and theology, had to begin from scratch, that a line had to be drawn through the history of many ages. A person had to bind himself independently to a new history. And with this new beginning, you could not make the work easier by calling on men of repute and authority. You had to act as though no one had ever thought about those questions and as though you had to start from nothing with them. The churches of the Reformation did indeed seek firm foundations [when considering] new problems and found this in the Bible as God's Word, but many thinkers from those days were also unwilling to recognize that authority unconditionally and had to rebuild things entirely and anew.

It is inherent to the character of this issue that such a radical revolution can never be entirely successful. It is impossible to ignore history continually without some form of process. Humanity does not have the power to free itself continually from all the considerations and thoughts that were dominant through previous ages. And even if one wanted to do that, it would not seem to be achievable. Even when one seems to have broken with all previous consultations and opinions, one remains unconsciously influenced by them—often incalculably so. Now we see all this very clearly indeed, but in those days people felt very differently. That era lacked a certain historical sense. People still lived under the naive presupposition that a human being or a people group had the power to wipe away the past and start [everything] afresh. Later, the same idea also enchanted the forerunners of the French Revolution. They also believed that one could draw a line under all that had gone before, fundamentally turn society upside down, and in all simplicity *retourner à la nature* ["return to nature"]. That idea also quickly turned out to be an illusion. Just as it was not possible for Rousseau[1] and his fellow agitators to transform society with a swish of the hand, it was also impossible for the Renaissance thinkers to neglect entirely the spiritual history of the Middle Ages. European thought is so deeply permeated by the foundational ideas of Christianity, both in its view of nature and in its considerations on marriage, morality, law, state, and so on, that violent efforts to cut ourselves loose of it seem foolish.

With all that, however, people in those days saw their task as that of making a new beginning. Then, though, people felt a great reticence. Where should one begin, and where should one end? If one may no longer call on the thinkers of former ages, where should one then begin? More starkly still, which method should one then follow? One could no longer descend deductively from the greater to the lesser because one was no longer certain about the greater. The greater basic premises themselves had been attacked and had begun to shake. Which path could still lead to certain knowledge? Where [could one find] the possibility of certainty, of firmness, of clear conviction? Those questions powerfully pushed themselves to the fore and gave European

---

1   Jean-Jacques Rousseau (1712–1778), a Genevan political philosopher.—Ed.

thought a particular direction from that time on. From now on, [the idea went,] one had to try to come to a doctrine of knowing [*kenleer*], to a method of knowing [*kenmethode*]. [One had to avoid] any beautiful reflections on the essence of things and the ground of things but very soberly and humbly ask oneself, "What can I know [*weten*]? What can I accept with certainty?"

In England, as we have seen, people felt attracted to the inductive method. There it was believed that in the very first place, one had to begin by perceiving things, to discover new things, to let eye [watch] and ear listen, to take up what is happening in the world around us. Alongside this, England also knew a more mystical, Neoplatonistically inclined movement, but that movement very much lacked philosophical foundations, [for which reason] it could not wield great influence. And as such, England remained the land of perception, of the study of nature, of empiricism.

In continental Europe, and specifically in France, one immediately sensed serious considerations against this empirical method. Faith in the reliability and certainty of sensory perception was not as strong there as in Britain. As well as this, it was thought that sensory perception can indeed teach us all manner of important things but that different facts nonetheless bear a more or less accidental character. Tomorrow, different and new perceptions can overthrow them. Through sensory perception, I can perceive that particular phenomena are *so* but not that they *must* be *so* or that they could not be *otherwise*. Therefore, according to the insight of the French thinkers, the knowledge that we gain through sensory perception is always an uncertain and random thing. Real philosophy cannot be built on it. Along with this, the question returned with renewed power, "How can we then gain certain knowledge?" The French philosopher gave the following answer: "In the same way that we come to certainty in mathematics. We must construct our philosophy analogously to mathematics. Only then will we stand on firm ground." While English thought began by forming an alliance with natural science, French [thought] wanted to orient itself more toward mathematics.

In the final instance, this notable difference points back to a difference in personality. The psychical balance is different in the empiricist and in the rationalist. In the empiricist, the functions of the soul are grouped more around the functions of perception, and in the rationalist, more around the connective [functions], around the thinking [functions]. The empiricist lives more from the outward in, and the rationalist more from the inside out. In one, the accent is placed on the outward-oriented processes, and in the other, the emphasis lies on the internal processes. They are undoubtedly different types of people who come to us in each of these worldviews. And with this, we see that the one never fully conquers the other, that they both constantly return everywhere in different forms!

We must consider the French philosopher René Descartes as the founder of this rationalism. In his youth, having been brought up in a Jesuit school, he quickly sensed his opposition to the deductive method followed there—from all sorts of basic premises accepted in advance, from Aristotle and the church fathers. In that time, he seems to have shown an exceptional capacity for the philosophical subjects. In his later philosophical development, he never severed his connection to the Roman church but always submitted to the great truths of the faith. This, in a certain sense, is striking when one follows how very much he moved down new paths.

In his investigation, Descartes proceeded from a certain skepticism toward all possible paths to knowledge. He considered deduction in the scholastic sense to be of little value. He wanted to build from the ground up. But he also had little trust for sensory perception. Who can actually assure us that we are not dreaming? How do we know with certainty that things are as we think we perceive them to be? In dreams, we also have the striking impression that we are dealing with people and things. Can we ever determine with certainty that in our waking moments we might as well be dreaming? Is it not possible that we inhabit a perpetual illusion? What sort of value should we then attach to sensory perception? The only method that offers us complete certainty is the mathematical.

The mathematical method proceeds from certain generally recognized axioms, which one can lay down as the foundation of all further investigation—and that with complete safety. From that, one can successively approach different truths and, as it were, can discover new truths and climb higher. One no longer revolves in a little circle of thoughts, as with the scholastic philosopher, but rather, one can progress further from one proposition to another. In this way, according to Descartes, we must also set to work in philosophy. Now with this naturally [comes] the question of which axioms we may take as the foundation for the whole. A great deal depends on this because one may not proceed on the basis of some arbitrary conviction or other. One must take as foundational only such a proposition that cannot be doubted, that must be accepted without proof. There can be no further discussion of that basic premise. It must be a solid foundation that can support the entire building.

For Cartesius,[2] much depended on which thought he would lay down as the foundation for his system. This is why he sought very cautiously and methodically until he believed himself to have found a certain foundation. He said, "In all my doubt and uncertainty, there is one thing that I cannot doubt, and that is that I am doubting, which is to say, that I am thinking."[3] I may be shaken and tossed around, but this one thing always remains certain to me, that I think and thus also [that I] am, [that I] exist. I think, therefore I am. *Cogito, ergo sum.* "Therefore this knowledge that I think and thus that I exist is the first and most certain of all [knowledge]."[4] Even if everything in the world should fail, I would still know [*weten*] and recognize with certainty that I doubt and thus also that I think and thus also that I must exist. Now that is not to say, as it were, that I deduce my existence through a logical process of reasoning from my thinking but rather that I recognize my existence

2   Here Bavinck uses the Latinized form of Descartes.—Ed.

3   Here Bavinck refers to René Descartes, *Discours de la méthode* (Leiden, 1637), part 4. For an English translation of this work, see Descartes, *A Discourse on the Method of Correctly Conducting One's Reason and Seeking Truth in the Sciences*, trans. Ian Maclean, Oxford World's Classics (Oxford: Oxford University Press, 2006), 28.—Ed.

4   Here Bavinck refers to Descartes, *Discours de la méthode*, part 4.—Ed.

through a simple mental intuition (*simplici mentis intuitu*). I think, therefore I am—that is the basic premise of Descartes's philosophy. My self-consciousness teaches me with immediate certainty that I exist.

In this basic premise, Descartes had very considerable intentions. He knew well that the great difficulty [faced by] our thinking is the leap from subject to object, from thinking to being. How can I deduce from my thinking that that which I think also really exists? With the world, I cannot make that leap from thinking to being, from subject to object. I imagine a world, but whether that world also exists cannot immediately, clearly, and certainly be proved from this. I must take the leap from thinking to being where it is at its very smallest, where thinking and being come together, and that is in my soul itself. I think, therefore I am. There thinking includes being. There thinking presupposes being. There the subject is also the object. I am always thinking of myself. I am conscious of myself. If we take that leap there, we are fully protected against illusions. I may doubt everything, but however much more I doubt, I experience all the more that in my doubting I am thinking and thus also must exist. However much more uncertain other things become, this is precisely the thing that becomes more certain.

It should be noted that the concept of "thinking" had a very broad meaning for Descartes. By this, he did not mean actually thinking *about* [things], but rather, he held together all the phenomena of consciousness within it. This is why we can then proclaim that the soul always "thinks," which then means that the soul always entails consciousness.

Now Cartesius failed to see that when considered in strictly logical [terms], the leap he took, however small it might be, was completely unacceptable. He believed that thinking, thinking of oneself, was sufficient grounds to accept that the soul exists substantially. I think, therefore I exist as a substance, as an independent being. This conclusion is doubtless [arrived at] too briskly. One can say, "I think, therefore my thinking exists." One can also say, "In my thinking there is always a distinctive 'I moment,' that idiosyncratic little pull of self-consciousness." But to deduce from this that there must also be a substantial soul, even to lay this conclusion as the foundation for all subsequent investigation, is a deed that is not fully guaranteed. Descartes proposed this too simply, too easily. On the most extremely difficult issues around self-consciousness, of the substantial soul, and so on, he leaped forward too easily and did not see that in doing so, he gave the rest of his system a foundation that was too weak to support the building.

In his subsequent considerations, Descartes constantly had to deal with the concept of the "substance." This is a concept that our thinking itself, in a certain sense, creates. We let ourselves think about everything in the world as substances with attributes. If I say, "Red," I immediately ask, "What is red?" because the attribute *red* can only be thought of as inherent to a substance. In the same way, thinking actually analyzes all phenomena. On its own, it can make abstract concepts into independent things for a moment, think [of them] as substances, and attribute all sorts of qualities to them. I can speak of the iron that is hard, of the virtue that is praiseworthy, of the righteousness that is glorious. I always place myself opposite the things to which I attribute qualities. Thinking analyzes all phenomena as substances and attributes. It is always occupied with [the task of] attributing certain predications to a particular subject.

A distinctive [feature] of this is that an attribute (*modus*) cannot be thought of on its own. A *modus* can never exist in a vacuum. It longs for the substance in which it rests. Our thinking can find no rest when it has identified only an attribute [because] it wants to apply that attribute to a particular substance. If I say, "Red," then I ask, "What is red?" If I say, "Friendly," then I ask, "Who is friendly?" Each attribute can be thought of only as resting in a substance. We could define it this way: an attribute is a phenomenon that always needs something in order to exist; it is something that can be thought of only in [relation to] something else.

If that is true, a substance must be something that needs nothing else in order to exist, that rests in itself, that can be thought of on its own. If that were not so, the substance would actually be an attribute. Then I would immediately have to ask, "What is the other thing that the substance needs in order to exist?" Only that other thing would then be worthy of the name "substance," of "independence." As such, we must put it this way: a substance is a thing that needs nothing else in order to exist. A substance is something that can be thought of as resting in itself. As soon as we say that, it is immediately clear that very many of the things that we handle for a moment as substances in our language—for example, friendliness—are not substances. Friendliness cannot be thought of as resting in itself. Rather, it needs someone who is friendly. Our language often handles all sorts of phenomena as substances that in reality are not substances. There are few real substances, and they can be brought back to a few groups. This entire concept of substance is not taught to us by sensory perception, but rather, it is created within our thinking itself and applied in every direction.

Among the attributes that have a substance, Cartesius made another distinction between essential attributes and incidental attributes. Essential attributes are those attributes that make up the essence of the substance. You cannot imagine them away without also imagining away the substance itself. That the chest standing before me is brown is arbitrary, that it is hard, is incidental. But that it is spatial, that it takes up a particular location, is not incidental. I cannot imagine a chest that does not take up a particular location. Its spatiality is an essential attribute, an attribute that pertains to all material things. In the same way, Cartesius recognized thinking as an essential attribute of the soul. All its other attributes are incidental, but thinking is an attribute of the mind [geest]. Not for one moment can I imagine it away. The soul is always thinking.

Descartes's system is built on all these considerations. We will not follow him in the further outworkings [of that system]. It will be enough for us to occupy ourselves with the idea that he believed he could think of all other substances from the soul. Before all others, [this entails] the substance that is God. The idea of God, of the existence of God, is innate to us. It lies in my soul like a treasure, and I can never lose that treasure. Therefore, I must hold most firmly to the existence of God.

Once we know [weten] with certainty that we ourselves exist, from ourselves, from our thinking, we can find the lines, as it were, that lead us to all other substances, God, and the world. In this way, Descartes believed himself able to overcome doubt and to find the solution to the great [existential] questions placed before us every day.

Rationalism, of which Descartes was the founder, reached its zenith on our own soil [i.e., the Netherlands] in the great thinker Baruch Spinoza. Spinoza was not actually solely a rationalist; he was also a mystic. His system includes different traits, and yet his philosophy is nonetheless a colossal unity. Few philosophers have wielded greater influence on the history of modern philosophy. At first forgotten and despised, this philosopher was later rediscovered, from which time his influence has steadily increased. Schleiermacher[5] lauded him as "Saint Spinoza." Goethe says of him that he "elevated himself to the pinnacle of thought, who to the present day seems to remain the standard of all speculative efforts."[6] It is not only that the capacity for thought was so great in him. As a human being, as a personality, he was also a great example to many. Cast out of his own circle, he worked toward his great task as a lonely and almost-never-understood [man] in quiet seclusion and unlimited humility. His depth, inwardness, and sharpness of mind compel all to amazement.

In many regards, Spinoza followed lines that had begun with Cartesius. He also wanted to build philosophy analogously to mathematics. Yes, he went further in this than his predecessor: his form also retained the mathematical method. His magnum opus, the *Ethics*,[7] is a notable and exemplary product of this philosophical method. Naturally, it is not possible for us to sketch out his system fully. For the time being, it will have to suffice for us to draw some of its lines.

Cartesius defined the concept of "substance" like this: it is something that needs no other thing in order to exist. The contrast with the concept of "attribute," *modus*, was adequately expressed in this [defini-

---

5   Friedrich Schleiermacher (1768–1834), Prussian theologian and polymath widely regarded as the father of modern theology.—Ed.

6   The original German reads, . . . *sich zu dem Gipfel des Denkens hervorgehoben, der bis auf den heutigen Tag nog das Ziel aller spekulativen Bemühungen zu sein scheint.*—Ed.

7   *Spinoza's Ethics*, trans. George Eliot, ed. Clare Carlisle (Princeton, NJ: Princeton University Press, 2020).—Ed.

tion] because a *modus* always needs something different in which it can rest. Spinoza proceeded from this definition but soon came to the conclusion that, taken strictly, there can be only one substance, namely, God. Only God needs nothing else in order to exist, and every other thing is dependent on him. God, then, is also the only and infinite substance that lies at the foundation of all being. Such a conclusion is not unexpected from Spinoza because Descartes had already more or less prepared it. Descartes himself had also proclaimed that only God could be thought of as a substance in the fullest sense (*Princ. Phil.* 1, 51).[8] But while Descartes recoiled from this consequence, Spinoza embraced it in its full value. And with this, obviously, a great revolution in worldview was set in motion. For Cartesius, in the first place it is the *I* that thinks of itself, that is sure of its own existence. For Spinoza, the accent falls entirely from the *I*, and from then on, the full emphasis falls on the existence of God.

If this is true, all other things must be looked at entirely differently. It is not actually *my* thinking, but rather, it is God's thought that thinks of itself in me, through me. And then, the idea of *Cogito, ergo sum* is also not the first truth. Rather, it is the beginning of every lie because I do not exist as a substance. As a being, I do not stand alone, depending on nothing. Then it is only the eternal God whose existence is expressed in my living and thinking, and then my god-consciousness [*godsbewustzijn*] is nothing else than a spark of his divine self-consciousness. And then I am nothing but a small wave in the ocean of divinity, a tiny spark in the fire, a *modus* of his infinite substance. In comparison to him, all things take on a derivative and shadowy existence. They no longer deserve the name "independent."

By the nature of things, in Spinoza, this is not a conclusion that he draws on the basis of all sorts of arguments but much more one [reached

---

8   Here Bavinck refers to Descartes's *Principia philosophiae* (Amsterdam: Ludovicum Elze-virium, 1644), part 1, sec. 51, in which Descartes argues that the term *substance* applies differently to God and to creatures in that God is not dependent on his creatures. For that reason, Descartes claims that there is "no clearly intelligible sense" of the term that applies both to God and to creatures.—Ed.

on the basis of] his whole character, which bends toward it. He was one of
the most religious figures in Western thought. The existence of God was
so immediately real and great to him that he had to see things this way.
God is the ultimate unity who distinguishes himself in endless shades,
who unfolds the richness of his being in an unlimited number of *modi*
[i.e., attributes]. Each thing may seem to be an independent [entity] that
rests in itself. We may even handle it as such for a moment, by way of
comparison. But ultimately, there is only one independent entity, and
each thing is only conceivable as existing in him.

Not every person is mighty enough in his thinking to penetrate
so far into things. It is possible for someone to remain in the world
of *modi*, so that one notices all sorts of laws between those *modi*, so
that one loses himself in the diversity. Then one draws lines from one
modus to the others, striding forth on the periphery. By using a couple
of peripheral points, you can reach another point on the periphery,
you can approach each different point. But all that knowing [*weten*]
remains superficial, peripheral, stuck in the diversity. One would do
better by drawing the line from the periphery to the center point, to the
ultimate unity who is all in all. Then, once and for all, a person has laid
bare the essence of things and has found unity and depth. And from
that center point, he can find his way to each point on the periphery.
That is not always possible for every person. Most people think [only]
of things, of themselves, of the *modi*. The real thinker approaches the
center, grasps deeper, and finds God as the only independent [being]
who lies at the foundation of all the *modi*. As soon as the human being
starts to think of God, as soon as his thinking approaches God, it is
God who thinks of himself in him. He blends, so to speak, into God
and comes to stand alongside God. That is the highest thinking that
stands before us as an ideal and that we can strive for with our strength.

Therefore, there are grades of knowledge, of thinking. In the first
place, there is lower knowledge, imagination, representation, which is
the sensory knowledge with which we perceive things, taken up within
us. This is passive, blinding, inadequate, misleading. It makes us stand
still by the form and not approach the essence, and [it keeps us] by

the multiplicity, never finding the unity. In the second place, there is reasonable knowledge, which discovers laws, which observes rational construction and marvels at it. The highest knowledge is *scientia intuitiva*, intuitive knowledge, which immediately considers the essence of things (*Ethics* 2, propos. 40, schol. 2).[9] [Through this,] the human being acquires an equivalent, an adequate knowledge of the highest being, the substance.

With regard to God, Spinoza posed the question, Which attributes—that is, which essential attributes—must be ascribed to him? Descartes had said that matter possesses the essential attribute of spatiality, and mind [the attribute] of thinking.

Spinoza did not believe in the independence of matter and spirit and considered them both forms of God's existence. For him, then, the form of the question changed, becoming, Which attributes must be ascribed to God? He answered this question with the following: God possesses an infinite number of essential attributes. The richness of his essence is so unspeakably great that only an unlimited number of attributes is able to give expression to that fullness. Of all these, our knowing can reach only thinking and spatiality. It is striking that Spinoza made use of experience here. That we know [*kennen*] only two attributes—namely, thinking and expansiveness—can be established only through experience. Logical demonstration does not teach us this. As such, we can observe it only as a fact. In his system, Spinoza incorporated an idea that can be learned only through experience and with this deviated from his rule that experience cannot actually serve as a source of knowledge because we have to build the truth only through logical construction.

Spinoza's whole system of thought is marked by uplifting beauty and depth. He provides a broad overview of [all that] happens and focuses [our] attention time and time again on the depth of the issues at hand. In him [we also see] great emotion for the unspeakable majesty of the divine being, which is the cause, the indwelling cause, of all existence.

9 Here Bavinck refers to Spinoza's *Ethica, ordine geometrico demonstrata* (1677), part 2, prop. 40, scholium 2. There Spinoza argues for intuitive knowledge alongside reason and imagination as forms of knowing.—Ed.

From this, all the lines move forward into life. This idea dominated [his] entire life view [*levensbeschouwing*] and is expressed most clearly in his ethics.

As long as a person lives in the semblance of things, still conceives of things as independent entities, and does not see that among them all God is the only independent entity, his life is still bound to nature. He remains pushed by the powers of nature, still lives passively, and is subject to the impressions that storm around him. His life remains on the periphery. He stares blindly at the laws and relations among the *modi*. His love remains directed toward external things, toward the world of phenomena. It is very well possible that he himself does not see this, because he still sees the world of phenomena as the only one that is real. Something in him must be broken through. He must step out of all those visible and ostensible things and come to insight in his own deepest being. He must become active in the highest sense and indulge himself according to his deepest existence. When a person becomes conscious of his being, of his essence, he also intuitively feels his unity with the divine independence. Then he senses that it is God himself who has pushed through the layers of passivity in his thinking and loving [in order that he might] come to self-consciousness. That is the highest life in activity. Activity is that a human being's life is no longer lived [by things beyond itself] but that he himself *lives*, not limited by impressions from outside but defining himself, no longer chasing after the varied phenomena outside himself but finding peace in the depths of his own soul. Activity is that a human being's essence comes to be expressed in his life. And what is the essence of a human being? That he is a *modus* of the eternal independence of God, that he has a part in God's existence, that God's thinking and loving proceed through his soul.

A person must pursue this, but it is often foreign and far removed in his life. Passive powers are often the ones that rule his life. The passivity of sensory perception exercises its influence in his living and feeling. But above all, the darker passions of his soul are those that drag him along, that carry him away from himself, that make him live the life of untamed desire in which the soul must feel itself foreign. Human life is pressed and bent, struck down and harried, dragged along and carried away. The human being is passive and undergoes this as his lot until this breaks open within him, until he comes to the great insight of all things in their essence, until he sees God himself as the only independent entity. Then the source of longing for the external appearance of things dries up within him, and he directs the fullness of his love toward God as the only being, as the essence of his essence. The human being thus often leads a slavish life, a life of passivity. This is because he is a phenomenon, a *modus*. As a *modus*, he sits squeezed between the other *modi*, the other phenomena that define him, just as the center point of a circle is squeezed between the other points. As soon as awareness of the [divine] essence is awakened within him, as soon as he draws the line to the center and points himself toward God, he becomes free, he lives the life of God, he loses all relativity. Now one cannot say that there is a single person who is only passive, who is only slavish, and one can no less say that there is a single person who is only active, who lives from God. In life, the active and the passive are wonderfully intertwined. The conditions of one often cross over unnoticed into the conditions of the other. We can indeed say, however, that the active must be considered the highest and that therefore all moral doctrine must be based on the idea that as a reasonable being, the human must know himself in God and love God with reasonable love.

The passive and the active thus stand opposite one another. For Spinoza, this does not mean that they must be thought of as an eternal contrast. Soul and body, spirit and matter are not a contrast because they both rest in God. In a human being, the passive sensory life is not a life from some demonic force, although it is a limited life. As long as a person proceeds into the world of the senses, he conceives of things as independent entities because he does not yet see them in God. That is not a devilish lie; rather, it is only an insufficient concept. He does not yet see all the elements but sees only the outward side and thus does not look purely. The passive life is also the life of God, is also rich and beautiful, but it is as yet confused. It does not yet see things in their deepest existence. The passive is not yet complete. It imposes limits, and as such it stands beneath the active, which sees eternity. Nonetheless, the power and law of God are at work in both, in the active and in the passive life, because all phenomena are [subject to] laws and happen "according to the necessity of the divine nature" (*Ethics* 1, prop. 29).[10] Spinoza thus recognizes a divine command that runs through everything. All things are as they must be, according to divine law: "Because when the human being understands the whole order of the world clearly, he would discover that everything is just as necessary as the things handled in mathematics" (*Cogitata metaph.* 2, c. 9, 2).[11]

As such, there is nothing random in life. You can approach everything logically [and see that] it is a mighty plan of thought. [This can also be said of] the gradual transition from the passive life lived [by things beyond itself] to the active [life], to perceiving that in the existence of the world, there is a necessary life growth. At the end of all thinking, the ideal image arises before us of seeing all things *sub specie aeternitatis*, in the light of eternity. Then all the bands that limit us fall away, and the human being sees himself and all things as resting in God. He then loves that God with an intellectual and an eternal love (*amor intellectualis et aeternus*, *Ethics* 5, 27),[12] which is the highest of all virtues. This true knowledge sets [him] free from all his heart's dark passions and lifts the human being above all his limitations and bondage.

It cannot be denied that Spinoza was one of the greatest thinkers of the modern age. Through tough patience, through refined feeling, and from reason, he built up a worldview [marked by] stunning simplicity

10 Here Bavinck refers to Spinoza's *Ethica, ordine geometrico demonstrata*, part 1, prop. 29, in which Spinoza argues that the divine nature exists by necessity, which in turn causes all things to exist and to exist in particular ways.—Ed.
11 Here Bavinck refers to Spinoza's *Cogitata metaphysica* (1663), part 2, chap. 9, prop. 2, in which Spinoza claims that all things are necessitated by the divine decree and that no single thing is necessitated by itself. As the complexity of this reality eludes human comprehension, however, Spinoza claims that we instead rely on a compensatory (but inadequate) distinction between some things as possible and others as necessary.—Ed.
12 Here Bavinck refers to Spinoza's *Ethica, ordine geometrico demonstrata*, part 5, prop. 27, in which Spinoza argues that the highest virtue and contentment of the mind is an intuitive knowledge of God.—Ed.

and depth. The worth of his system also rises higher because he was not only a thinker; he was also a mystic who proceeded from the beneficent warmth of his thoughts.

Despite this, on many fronts, all manner of critique came forth. This criticism dealt with four points.

In the first place, Spinoza forgot that in his system he constantly took up ideas that could not be drawn from logical deduction but rather only from experience. The corresponding existence of matter and spirit is not something that thinking can create according to the insights of logic but rather something that is taught to us by experience. That is a truth that we come to through induction, not deduction. No less is it possible to arrive at the oneness of substance from the multiplicity of the *modi*. The leap from unity to multiplicity is not one that can simply be made through logical construction. The necessity of the multiplicity can never be deduced from the unity. If someone believes in the multiplicity, he does so because he cannot observe [reality] differently. That is an experiential truth. In no single regard is it given to logical, necessary proof. Spinoza's system has the appearance of building a worldview from a few definitions, just as mathematics is built from axioms. In reality, [though,] ideas that we can only know through experience creep between all those subtle, logical considerations, and Spinoza cannot possibly prove that as logical. No one can prove the existence of a material and spiritual world by logical deduction from the existence of God. Nor can anyone make clear the necessity of the existence of the multiplicity of things from the existence of God. In the midst of all these propositions and proofs gathered together by Spinoza, there are always clumps of experience, clumps of reality that are made known to us only by perception.

A second—and no less earnest—objection to Spinoza's system is that he took the leap from thinking to being too easily. At most, we might be able to conclude that our thinking leads naturally to the concept of "God," that we must necessarily conceive of the concept of God. Even if one agreed with Spinoza on all the rest, one could still go no further than this idea: that our thinking must necessarily think of one substance that exists in infinitely many attributes. But then the question remains: How can I ever arrive at reality? Who can assure me that my thinking is objectively valid, that what I think is indeed so? Rationalism teaches logical intent, the reasonableness of things, but leaves us standing before the question of the reality of things. On the basis of one, how can I reach a decision on the other? The leap from thinking to being is extremely difficult and dangerous. One may not take it without great care. Now this issue did not exist in the same way for Spinoza because he was deeply convinced of the existence of God. He was not only a rationalist but also a mystic. The existence of God was so obvious to him that he could incorporate it without saying a word.

No less serious is the concern that mystery has no place in Spinoza's system. With him, everything is logical. One thing follows after another. It cannot be otherwise. One thing must be like this and the other like that. At all manner of points, Christianity accepted mystery and rested in it. On the question of why God created the world, why God created it so, [Christianity] answered with mystery. We believe it, but we cannot probe its depths. Mystery—not at all as irrational but rather as suprarational, certain—is the inscrutable [reality] that we may not approach with our little ideas. In Spinoza's system, mystery is resolved. Everything is rational and necessary. There is something oppressive in such an idea, something stifling, something that strikes the human being dead. [Indeed,] mystery is where he ultimately finds rest; he can wrestle with it, but finally he bows down before it. In it, he is reminded of his smallness and of the great majesty of God. We can only think a small part of [God's] eternal thoughts after him, but we can never plumb their deepest depths. Thoroughgoing rationalism comes on us like a specter who grinds the intricate puzzles of creation and life between his rigid fingers and fills life and death with angst.

The fourth objection goes along with this: Spinoza's system does not do justice to personality. What actually remains of the human being? His life is struck dead by the idea of mathematical necessity. His existence itself is dissolved, evaporated, into a *modus*, a phenomenon. That which is real in his life, his love and hate, his seeking and longing, lose their tingling warmth and their life-giving reality. Everything becomes contrived, a logical process. You feel yourself sucked out of life into the sphere of viewing, from which you can see all things as risible, as unreal. Personality is indeed nothing more than a flighty connection between *modi*, and the fermentation process between the *modi* is what we call "life." For Spinozism, there was also no place for history. The life and work of history, the unique [i.e., the one-off occurrence, *het Einmalige*] in all its worth, the growth of peoples and of their cultures, in short, history itself entirely lost its essence in Spinozism. It crumpled all events together until they fell apart as *modi* of the only independent entity.

And so, from all these sides, objections had to burst forth. For many, rationalism led to skepticism. It was inevitable that this bridge of reason would wreak revenge. Life itself had to slash [rationalism's] binding cords to pieces. At first, this skepticism remained limited while [Spinoza's] mystical tendencies continued to take effect. For example, Pascal[13] was a great thinker who broke with rationalism and found peace in mysticism. He believed in the heart, in the knowledge of hearts, which goes beyond rational knowledge. "Reason's final step is knowing that there is an infinity of things that surpasses it."[14] "The heart has its reasons that reason does not know: one feels it in a thousand things. It is the heart that feels God, and not reason."[15] It is the heart that can feel the presence of God, where thinking is impotent to climb up toward him.

Among others, this skepticism took on much more serious forms. Doubt toward the existence of things, toward the certainty of reason, toward the existence of God, arose on every side. Life itself grew and knocked over the fences put in place by reason in its overconfidence. How can we ever gain certainty about reality? That question remained

13 Blaise Pascal (1623–1662), a French polymath and Catholic theologian.—Ed.
14 The original French reads, *La dernière démarche de la raison, c'est de connaître qu'il y a une infinité de choses qui la surpassent.*—Ed.
15 The original French reads, *Le coeur a ses raisons que la raison ne connaît point: on le sent en mille choses. C'est le coeur qui sent Dieu et non la raison.*—Ed.

as a fearful complaint, a complaint felt by many as a need in their lives. Rationalism could not meet that need.

When we look at this development from afar, and especially when we do so with an eye to the issue of personality, it becomes clear to us that in its deepest essence, rationalism was a grasping, an intuition, a worldvision. It was a becoming conscious of personality but then of that personality in which the center was placed in the inward processing functions. In rationalism, a type of human expresses himself. Behind rationalism there lies the secret of a personality.

That seems to be so from different traits. Before all else, [it is seen in] the remarkable way balance is found. For rationalism, there is no sensory perception, no receptivity, and also no feeling, no will. Everything is traced back to reason, to thinking. The soul's only attribute is thinking, the inner process. That is a very characteristic trait. The psychical life's full accent is laid on the inward functions, on the powers of reason, the connections. Through this, the psychical balance is skewed to one side. The whole bows too strongly in one direction; one function overgrows all the others. In this worldview, this is as clear as the light of day.

A second trait in which this is seen is rationalism's helplessness in life. It is timid. It remains a viewer, watching life's great powers with amazement, and stays watching from outside. You find that trait in many people who do not really take part in life, like bystanders watching and taking account [of life]. Rationalism remains foreign to life. It can never take the leap from viewing to doing. Therefore, while this worldview is so exciting in the lecture hall, it melts away beneath you in the loud marketplace that is life.

And that is only looking at it in a purely psychological way. We can also approach it differently. Rationalism attaches exceptional value to the active, inner function, to thinking. It builds a world system like a beautiful mosaic, with no other details (at least, that is what it intends!) than the creations of reason themselves. The soul builds a world system from itself, without making use of passive experience, from the spontaneous power of its reason. That is an incomprehensibly strong accent on the soul's spontaneous, creative power. The soul has the power to free itself from all passive experience and construct a worldview solely from within itself. But if the soul can do that, yes, then it is a god. It can do what God does, what God did. Then you think up a world from within yourself just as God thought of a world from within himself. Then [the soul] itself is god; it is divine and regal. Then it is a spark of God, and its thinking is God's thinking. Pantheism is not the conclusion of rationalism, but it is its presupposition. Reason only has such power when it is itself god.

Even in this, [though,] there is great truth. The active, the regal, is undoubtedly a side of our existence. In all our science, we are much more creative than empiricism had ever assumed. Our thinking can proceed creatively, can find new paths, can track down necessities that far exceed experience in its entirety. But we must immediately add to this: it may be a side of our being, but it is not the only side. Alongside the creative activity of reason lies [our] great dependence. We tread forward into the world with questions, dependently. In each thing in our lives, we are also passive; we must listen to what the world beyond us is saying. Experience brings us into contact with multiplicity and unity, with matter and spirit. Experience leads us from knowledge to knowledge. Sometimes, once we have perceived [something], we can later show through logical deduction that it must also be so, but mostly experience goes first. We step passively into the world and must listen, alongside our thinking, and also perceive in our thinking.

The same is true in every area. We cannot think of God, cannot ascend to him with our thinking. Here we are also much more passive than rationalism had thought. We must listen to his voice, which permeates our lives. We are also passive in our life. We cannot think up norms from within ourselves, the great moral standards with which we deal. In this, we are also much more passive than rationalism claimed. We must listen to the voice of God, which comes to us in many ways. There is no single thing in which we are only creative or that we can bring forth only from within ourselves. Everywhere, passivity arcs through our lives. That passivity is not just something that clings to us as imperfection; rather, it is indispensable to us. It is an integral part of our existence.

Rationalism only emphasizes the functions [dealing with] inner activity. Through this, it pulls the personality apart and rips the unity of the soul. What it leaves behind is no longer a human being, a living and feeling human being, but rather a dull abstraction.

The human soul is both active and passive. In its most passive functions, it is still active. But in its most active creations, it is also passive and dependent on the things that happen to it. The human soul is simultaneously creative and receptive, small and great. Those two do not cancel each other out, but rather, they affirm one another. They demand and complete each other. It is precisely when a person steps into the world with questions and with a sense of his dependence that he can become conscious of the immeasurable riches that he carries within him in his reason. When he asks questions of life and the world, receptively, he is always greater than he assumes. That also applies to a person in every area, in every sphere of life. It is when someone is aware that in the deepest spiritual questions he is also dependent on divine light and asks for and seeks this that he becomes rich. This is when his personality remains firm; it remains in one piece. In his smallness he remains great; in his receptivity [he remains] a king.

Neither empiricism nor rationalism has plumbed the depths of personality. It is not only receiving or only creating. It is not only slavishness or kingliness. It is being a small and dependent and sinful creature and yet also belonging to God's family. It is that God is immanent within a person and is yet also transcendent far above him. It is being captive to lies and error and yet also to a certain extent remaining an image bearer of God. It is the mystery of smallness and greatness, of not [seeing] these two as an irreconcilable antithesis. Rather, [it is hearing] these two chiming together as one!

6

The Reaction of the Conscience

AT SOME POINTS IN HISTORY, life seems to have gone by far more quickly—when hearts were filled with strong emotions, great ideals, and high expectations. The turn of the eighteenth to the nineteenth century was one such time.

In those days, it seems that people were captivated by an entirely new mood. There was something revolutionary in the spiritual atmosphere. [That era] was dominated by a kind of electricity, a kind of tension that could be expected to burst forth at any moment. Undoubtedly, all this points out that we are dealing with one of those wondrous and noteworthy transitions in the history of the mind [*geestesgeschiedenis*] that usher in new cultural periods.

The revolutionary mood that we meet here goes much deeper and further than one might have first thought. It was not only related to state order and did not only aim at a civil and social revolution. It strove for far greater things [than these] and wanted to express itself in much greater things. It wanted to turn life upside down. It wanted to free [life] from the laws laid down beyond and above [us] and wake up life itself in its freedom and power. And through that, it wanted to revolutionize all of life. It related to each of life's phenomena and brought drastic changes to bear over the whole [of life].

In order to understand these things better, we must also look beyond the history of philosophy, [although] we must indeed deal in particular with this. For the sake of brevity, we must indeed limit ourselves to a few phenomena. In the first place, then, we wish to point out further the character of the distinctive mood [found in] English literature. The English poets and writers of those days actually all had a revolutionary quality. They all break with something and want to see new things being built. Nowhere do we find this more strongly than with Lord Byron,[1] who must certainly be considered one of the leading minds of those days. What is the revolution that comes to such fierce expression in this poet? In the first place, it is not resistance against social order; it does not aim only at political or social upheaval. It goes much deeper and is in essence much more capacious. It is a reaction against the morality, the religion, against the whole way of life of the previous generation. The sense of being shackled to fixed laws and silly rules, the prudishness and properness, that bound and established life on every side, the treadwheel[2] of polite considerations—this powerful poet broke from and ridiculed all these. The [kind of] polite civility that knew no greater misery than losing face and being ashamed, that in every act of life asked itself ten times over, "What will people say?" and that almost always honors and follows the honor [given by] others—this is what he attacked and wanted to rip to shreds, in order to be able to claim the freedom of life. And he also aimed at more than this. In him, we find opposition to the general recognition of laws and norms that are laid from outside ourselves. He was driven by the fierce and warm desire to construct his [own] life according to his own insight, according to his own power. It was a revolution not simply against propriety and civility but against every law and norm in general. In him, the untamable pull of freedom found its mouthpiece. A rebellious tone resounds through all his poems. In his stories, the heroes break from all norms, live out the great freedom of their own insights, and then perish—but even in their tragic deaths, they are great and wonderful. In all his works, you hear the effervescence of life itself, which rubs against the dams of laws and norms, which asks for

---

1   George Gordon Byron (1788–1824), a poet who stood at the forefront of the English Romantic movement.—Ed.

2   The treadwheel is a now-antiquated form of a human-powered engine.—Ed.

free development in every direction. And as such, the song of rebellion began in England, the Romantic song of life's desire to be unleashed.

You will find and experience the same mood if you take French art into account. Before you, you will see the styles of Louis XV and Louis XVI,[3] rococo art, with its pleasing, curled lines, with its intricately formed shells and softly rounded shapes. It is all so delicate, so fragile, so convivial. You must think of the shepherds and shepherdesses of the noble classes in those days, so cozily and subtly imitating the simplicity of outdoor life, but in that imitation you feel the unnaturalness and contrivance of that period. You feel yourself taken along into the salons of that era's great [thinkers], and you listen in on the charmingly warm discourse with which the thinkers battle one another. They launch their bold opinions—dangerous world-and-life views—but in their hands those worldviews are no sticks of dynamite. They are only balls thrown in a friendly game. You feel it: this is not life; it is pleasant chitchat that wants to discuss heaven and earth, that touches on everything, but only to elicit a smile from the beautiful woman around whom the thinkers are gathered. Fine curled lines, everything counted, measured out exactly—it is a game of refined beauty. In the middle of that gathering, you feel the need to hear the dull rumble of life itself—the life that can sometimes pour itself out in fire and destruction. In the midst of all those softly rounded lines and shells, you once again long to find the powerfully drawn straight line of the mighty will. You wait for a rebellious cry that sounds out the majesty of life itself, which is far more than pleasant discourse.

You hear that cry of rebellion in the mighty sounds of the French Revolution. The nice little balls thrown around with smiles became sticks of dynamite. In one strike, they destroyed the order of society itself. The Revolution's "boom" was like the release of massive, weighed-down powers that had to burst out at some point. In Napoleon,[4] the

---

3 Louis XV (1710–1774) and Louis XVI (1754–1793), the last two kings of France before the French Revolution.—Ed.
4 Napoleon Bonaparte (1769–1821), the French military leader who led France as first consul from 1799 to 1804 and as emperor from 1804 to 1814.—Ed.

great conqueror, you find that power and majesty. The age of soft, curved lines was alien to him.

If you want to look further, listen to the songs of Goethe's *Faust*— even if only those words with which Faust wanted to rerender the first portions of the Gospel of John: "In the beginning was the deed!"[5] Not reason, nuanced consideration, intellectual calculation, the carefully calculated estimation; it is the deed, the living, mighty deed, that stands behind all the phenomena in the world. In that deed there is something mysterious, often something unreasonable, something irrational, often something tragic, but it is always great and regal because behind that deed is life, which gives birth to the deed. There is tension, power, majesty in this [idea].

You can look at that era in all its forms and phenomena, and in every place you will find the same moods, the same revolutionary thoughts. You will see the life of that time expressing itself in its full reality in Beethoven's[6] passionate, powerful sonatas. You can best understand the transition from the eighteenth to the nineteenth century from one idea: life itself reacts against subtle considerations and refined forms. Life itself rubs against these dams and wants to break them. Therefore, at every point, and in every place, it is the song of rebellion against all propriety, against all order and authority, that captures every heart.

Every era needs its thinker, its philosopher, to give shape and depth to the powers at work within it. It was also so in the age of revolution, which sought its [own] thinker and found him in Immanuel Kant. In that time, many movements and inclinations were at work that found their classical formulations in him. He stands at the forefront of the modern age. Few minds have had more influence on the entire spiritual formation of the previous century than this intellectual hero. This is why it is simply impossible to ignore him. Whoever wants to understand our modern age must always be familiar with him to some degree. He was not the philosopher of refined discourse, not the one

5   The original German reads, *Im Anfang war die That!*—Ed.
6   Ludwig van Beethoven (1770–1827), German composer and pianist.—Ed.

throwing balls [in a game]. Rather, he was the thinker of [real] life, the philosopher who heard and understood the storm of his time and who wanted to look for firmness and strength, freedom and obligation, in new foundations.

To try to give a short overview of this exceptional philosopher's philosophical system is no simple task. Even more than before, we very much have to limit ourselves and can provide the major lines [of thought] only in sketch form.

In the first place, it should be noted that Kant brought a [form of] reconciliation between the two directions previously discussed— empiricism and rationalism. In his judgment, the human mind is neither only passive nor exclusively active. We do not receive all [our] knowledge from our sensory perception. That cannot be so because experience teaches us all sorts of factualities but no necessities. It gives us much material but no form. We may, however, no less build up an entire worldview from our reason itself. Reason does acquaint us with the form, but it gives no content to that form. It teaches us nothing regarding the actual existence of things. It is only when both are together that they are able to give us valuable knowledge.

Our soul is influenced by sensory perception. Impressions from beyond ourselves work themselves into us. We are subject to something. These impressions only acquaint us with phenomena, with appearances [Erscheinungen]. In that sense, our knowledge is given to us from outside [ourselves]. Now with this, it is by no means the case that the soul simply takes these impressions up into itself and changes nothing in them. To the contrary, from the outset, the soul is busy doing just that. The soul is active in its perceiving. In what does this activity consist? This, namely, that the soul orders those external experiences in its *aprioristic* ways of viewing [Anschauungsformen]: time and space.

At first glance, that might sound very strange. Kant, however, believed that space and time themselves were not concepts that were given to us through sensory perception. If that were true, if we could only know time and space through sensory perception, then we could also think them away. Everything that I perceive, I can also think away.

I can very well imagine that the chest standing over there did not stand there. [Such an imagining] does not in the least contain any conflict for my intuition. After all, sensory perception teaches us only factuality, not necessity. Sensory perception cannot teach us that the chest *must* stand there. It can make known only the existence of the thing itself. Now with time and space, this is all very different. If necessary, if I close my eyes, I can imagine away the existence of the world, but then in my thoughts, all that remains is an endless, empty space. It is impossible for me to think away that space, and each effort to do so must ultimately fail. Space is a necessary thing for our intuition. If there were nothing else, I would still always have to believe that space was there. This alone already proves that the concept of space cannot be based on experience because I can imagine away everything that experience teaches me. The same is equally applicable to time. Time is more a reflective form of viewing [*Anschaaungsform*], of the "inner sense" [*inneren Sinn*]. Time and space are both necessary and cannot possibly be thought of as not existing. This all demonstrates that they are not the products of arbitrary perception but are inherent to our knowing [*kennen*] itself. They are *aprioristic* forms of viewing [*Anschauung*] that precede experience. The soul enters the rich world of phenomena with both of these forms [in place] and orders its experiences therein. In each perception, the soul is thus simultaneously active and passive. It is never a mirror that only reflects that which comes to it from outside.

The path toward knowledge is not entirely abandoned with this perceiving. The soul goes much further than that. It also tries to classify external impressions, to trace out the relationships between them, and so forth. In short, a whole process of thought begins, which wants to push this work forward. In that work, the soul is not just a passive replica [of the impressions it receives]. It has its own laws. The intellect works its material into its own forms. Kant had great difficulty with tracking down the forms of the intellect. From the beginning, it was clear to him that there were more of these than with perception. There were not just two [of them], although he counted no fewer than twelve.

Here he used the well-known table of judgments,[7] which he applied in a completely different sense. Just as perception has common and necessary forms that carry along our nature, as it were, *a priori*, our intellect also has common laws according to which it must set to work. He calls these forms of thinking "categories." The notable thing about categories is that they are universally applicable, that we apply them in every area. Here a single example can serve to clarify this [point]. One of the categories is that of number. The intellect judges all things from the universal viewpoint of number. Whether we are speaking about virtues or peoples, about character traits or trees, we can apply the category of number everywhere. We cannot think of things other than in the form of quantity. Another category is that of substance. Wherever thinking has to deal with phenomena, it is inclined to think of a substance behind them. In a certain sense, it cannot do without this. The idea of substantiality is a necessary one, from which our intellect cannot possibly detach itself. The same also applies to causality. We cannot imagine it away. With every phenomenon, we will ask ourselves, "What is its cause?" Everything must have a cause. Causality is also not a product of experience, because experience teaches us that certain phenomena always take place after others, but it can never, ever demonstrate the necessity thereof. The idea of causality is thus a category, a form of thinking with which we work on external impressions and with which we order them. In that manner, Kant knew different categories, which he regarded as "conditions of thought" [*Bedingungen des Denkens*].

We need to understand Kant's ideas clearly. Kant does not teach that from birth, the human soul carries with it well-worn [*fix und fertig*] concepts of time and space, substance and causality. To the contrary, it is indeed very possible that led by sensory perception, the intellect first comes to the formulation of these great categories. But Kant teaches

7 Kant's table of judgments refers to the ways in which humans think of a particular thing as having certain attributes. The table has four categories, each of which has three judgments: quantity (universal, particular, singular), quality (affirmative, negative, infinite), relation (categorical, hypothetical, disjunctive), and modality (problematic, assertoric, apodictic).—Ed.

that these concepts themselves far transcend the intellect because they do not limit themselves to the observation of factualities but to the laying down of necessities. They are forms of our intellect, which is indeed first awakened, as it were, by experience but that is as such inherent to our thinking.

In the second place, in observing all these universal forms, nothing about reality is [actually] established. Do time and space exist? Do causality and substantiality exist? Do they exist outside myself? The intellect can never reach a verdict on these [questions]. We can never go further than to establish that our intellect must necessarily apply itself—according to these forms of viewing [*Anschauungsformen*] and categories—to all the impressions that flow toward us from outside [ourselves]. Each question about the reality that is external to me is inadmissible. We can never give an answer—we could only do so by crawling out of our own intellect. Our intellect is so [composed] that we can never see differently. To meet the reality that is objective, that counts independently of me, I would have to rid myself of all these forms and stand outside my own soul. And that, ultimately, is impossible. This is why we cannot even pose the question—a question that is also not urgent for us.

Now we could end the process of our knowing with this. We could be satisfied by observing that we receive impressions from outside; that these impressions make us know the appearances [*Erscheinungen*] [of things]; that we do not receive these impressions completely passively but that we immediately work on them according to the forms of perception [*Anschauungsformen*] and categories; that our image of the world [*wereldbeeld*] is thus composed of different elements, some of which we receive passively and others that we contribute *a priori*; [that] how the reality outside ourselves—with the "thing in itself" [*Ding an sich*]—is composed cannot easily be pursued. This, in short, would be the summary of our considerations. But Kant felt keenly that we are not satisfied with such. Thinking goes further, does not limit itself to these still quite simple concepts, and wants to penetrate deeper and further. That is a very wondrous trait in our thinking. "Reason is driven by a natural tendency to go beyond the use of experience, and, by means of mere ideas, dares venture beyond the extreme limits of all knowledge."[8] Our thinking always goes further; [it] climbs ever higher. And so we stride forth toward metaphysics.

There too it is thinking that necessarily leads to certain concepts. Thinking has the impulse to [move from] the relative to reach conclusions about the absolute, [to move from] the sensory to the eternal. It ascends to the very loftiest ideas of God, the soul, and the coherence of the world. In actual fact, by doing so, it takes an unauthorized leap. The forms of our intellect are always suitable for use on the appearances [Erscheinungen] [of things], on impressions localized in time and space, but they lack any capacity to acquaint us with that which is supersensory, spaceless, and eternal. Despite this, our reason cannot rest until it has pushed through the causes into the very first cause. It must remain on the terrain of the experiential and may not take a leap into the eternal. The fact that it must remain there, however, is not accidental. Rather, it rests on [reason's] entire nature. It is in reason's nature to want to reach conclusions on the very highest ideas. Those ideas are, as it were, ideals that it wants to approach. It could not rest in the relative but—according to the drive of its very nature—must move forward to that which is higher. Now it is obvious that the worth of such conclusions is very minimal. By the way, it also seems that whenever reason ventures onto the terrain of metaphysics, it constantly contradicts itself, always confuses itself in all manner of contradictions—a proof, indeed, that it cannot actually venture there. It cannot venture beyond the appearances [Erscheinungen] [of things]. Wherever it proceeds, where it climbs upward, it ends up confused by many, many problems.

This is why metaphysics, in its entirety, is so unfruitful. That applies to materialism just as much as to pantheism. It applies to all dogmatic systems. All these try to acquire some knowledge of the highest things

---

8   The original German reads, *Die Vernunft wird durch einen Hang ihrer Natur getrieben über den Erfahrungsgebrauch hinaus zu gehen, und vermittelst bloszer Ideën zu den auszersten Grenzen aller Erkenntnis hinaus zu wagen.* Immanuel Kant, *Kritik der reinen Vernunft* (Leipzig: Reclam, 1878), 605.—Ed.

with all manner of logical conclusions but forget that our intellectual categories are no longer to be used [on them] because we may direct them only to impressions that can be localized in time and space. The absolute, that which carries on eternally, is denied to us. We must humbly limit ourselves to that which can be experienced. With this, Kant notes very correctly that from his standpoint, it is equally impossible to teach that there is no God and that there is a God. Both claims are equally "dogmatic," equally inadmissible. We do not have sufficient grounds for one conclusion or the other.

As such, there is something tragic in the whole structure of our reason. It has an undeniable drive to ascend to the very highest but is unfit for that task. That is the tragedy of reason, which has given rise to so much striving and confusion.

Thus far, the result of Kant's philosophy is more or less negative. He had a very distinct intention, however, in these negative conclusions. In Kant's philosophy, the center of gravity does not lie in his theoretical considerations but rather in his practical foundations. His *Critique of Pure Reason* was thus followed by the *Critique of Practical Reason*, where [we find] that which is typical of his philosophy.

According to Kant, we are so composed that we proceed through life from certain *aprioristic* foundations, which are of great value to our whole approach to life. Life has its own laws, its own foundations; life has its own *a priori*, and with it we must face its great events. We do not prove these, but we proceed on their basis. We cannot imagine them away. Life's first foundation is the moral norm, the "thou shalt" [*du sollst*].

The content of this "thou shalt" [*du sollst*] might differ among people groups and individuals. One might treat as sin what another finds acceptable. This also goes along with upbringing and circumstances of all sorts. But the notable thing is that every human being knows [*kent*] such a "thou shalt." Every human being accepts as self-evident that he may not simply do anything, that he is subject to norms, to laws. Every person accepts this immediately. That is the *aprioristic* presupposition with which he treads into life. Every person who has done wrong also knows [*weet*] that he could have acted differently.

He naturally moves through life with this presupposition. That is the *a priori* of practical reason.

The idea of the "thou shalt" is sustainable only when there is a corresponding "thou art able" [*du kannst*], that is, when the soul is free in its acting. As soon as we believe that the soul is driven by the laws of causality, we lose the possibility of a moral norm. I can believe in a norm only when I sense that I am free to follow that norm—or not to follow it. Practical reason proceeds on the basis of belief in the freedom of the soul.

From this idea, practical reason ascends to the ideas of God and immortality. The "thou shalt" is, after all, a high demand, a task that the soul cannot simply fulfill but that can only be reached "in infinite progress" [*nur in einem ins Unendliche gehenden Progressus*]. Belief in immortality lies enclosed within this. In our lives, we must proceed arbitrarily from the idea of immortality because otherwise, life itself would be worthless. Life does give us the fulfillment of the highest norms, which are themselves grounded in life itself and can be considered only a fragment. It is only in this way that [life] is meaningful, that we can be reconciled to it. And only in that case can we recognize the norm as absolute.

As soon as we believe that, however, we must also obviously conclude for the existence of God. God is, as it were, "causality's moral disposition" [*der moralischen Gesinnung gemäsze Kausalität*]. He is the one who balances out virtue and happiness, evil and punishment. In him, all moral norms find their solid ground, because we recognize them as divine commands. By this, we must not think that we have reached a conclusion on the existence of a God on the basis of reasonable arguments for the existence of the freedom of the soul, and so on. All reasoning on these things is actually impossible because our thinking is not suited to it. It is the case, however, that as living human beings, as people who must act and work in every moment, we naturally postulate the existence of freedom, immortality, and God. In life, we proceed on that basis, [even if] wordlessly, because if we did not do so, life would lose its meaning and value to us. They form the *a priori* of life. We could not live without the presupposition—regardless of whether it has been defined—that we are free, that justice is at work, and that this life can be considered only a fragment.

Does life have any right to postulate this? May we attach any value to it? It is beyond doubt that we would not be allowed to if other considerations required us to accept that there is no God, no immortality, and no freedom. As we have already noted, however, we do not wholly arrive at these things with our theoretical thinking. Theoretical thinking can prove neither that God exists nor that he does not. This is precisely where practical reason plays the decisive role. Practical thinking demands the existence of God. Life demands it, and therefore we must direct our lives with that belief.

When we look at these different ideas in relation to each other for a moment, it strikes us immediately that Kant did indeed bring about a great revolution in philosophical thinking. You see this best when you compare his manner of holistic thinking with, for example, that of empiricism or rationalism. The empiricist proceeds from the idea of causality and is inclined to apply that idea to every domain of what happens in the world—and thus, also the life of the soul. He will say, "The soul is a machine. In all its processes, the soul is subject to the laws of causality, is moved along by the wave that is the self-same laws." "Yes," you will say, "but the soul always has the intuition that it is free. It acts but has the intuition that it could also have acted differently. It thinks that its deeds and thoughts are not unambiguously limited by all powerful laws but that it can freely define what it itself wants." Then the empiricist will say, "That is a mirage, an illusion. The soul thinks that it is free, but it is not free. That is self-deception. There is only mechanical causality. The human being is a machine." Empiricism reasons in this way. In fact, the whole Enlightenment reasons in this way. Kant breaks this idea because he wants to give life a place alongside thinking. Kant says, "Thought is not capable of determining with unshakable certainty that the substantial soul does not exist, that all psychical processes are thus mechanical processes in which causality reigns. Whenever thought wants to do this, it moves onto terrain that is forbidden to it. It must recognize that it cannot say anything with certainty on those most elevated of subjects." By pushing thought back, refusing its [attempt] to usurp power, Kant retains a place for faith. Now he can say, "Is it really true that life proceeds intuitively from the idea of freedom, of the moral norm? And if that is true, we must not allow that faith [in the idea of freedom] to be supplanted by the immature speculations of theoretical thought. In the name of life [itself], we must hold our courage in believing in that freedom."

The same also applies to the existence of God. In the past, and with angst-ridden efforts, people tried to prove the existence of God. In response to those arguments, others tried to prove that no God could exist. Kant says, "All this is folly." He shows that all those so-called proofs for the existence of God are no proofs [at all] but that, to the contrary, each effort to demonstrate his nonexistence must necessarily fail. Religion must be brought back from the sphere of speculation to the sphere of life. You could say, "A God *must* exist because otherwise, my life would be meaningless; because otherwise, the holiest thing I possess, that is, the intuition of being a moral being, would be taken from me. My heart says to me, a God must exist. I admit that sober thinking will not stand aside for such an argument—and may possibly laugh at it. But that sober thinking must then understand well that it has nothing to say on those things, that it is impotent in reaching a conclusion on such things." You say, "Yes, but I do not intuit that I am a moral being, [in which case] you cannot possibly prove the existence of a God to me." Then you must do it without God. But you must understand this: in all the storms and temptations of his life, as soon as a human being first comes to the thought that there is a moral law that resides within him and that commands him, then he must immediately believe implicitly in the freedom of the soul, in God, and in immortality—even if in a poorly reasoned and thin way. That is the *a priori* on which moral life is built.

It is precisely in this idea that you hear the sounds of that era. That era recovered respect for life. Pluizer,[9] who had dashed all morality

9   Here Bavinck refers to Pluizer, a character who symbolized scholarly materialism in the important late nineteenth-century Dutch literary work *De Kleine Johannes*. See

and faith into pieces, was relegated to a corner, as the heart reclaimed its rights. [That age] once again dared to postulate: "It *must*! I cannot possibly accept that that moral intuition within me is a lie, that my freedom is an illusion, that the holiest thing I possess as a human being should be folly."

If that all is true, it includes [the claim] that religion and science can never again come into conflict. When science remains science, which is to say, [when science] limits itself to those fields on which it has a right to speak, where the intellect, with its forms, may approach the material provided by the senses, that science can never claim anything that is disadvantageous or unwelcome to religion. They have completely different terrains. Science deals only with the field of the appearances [*Erscheinungen*] [of things], of the relative. From the outset, religion deals with freedom, the absolute, and the eternal. Thinking cannot even approach these concepts, let alone overthrow them. Religion and science can work alongside one another fraternally. Science deals only with pure thought, and religion, to the contrary, is rooted only in the heart, in practical thinking, in life. With this, religion also falls out of the sphere of evidence, where it is otherwise daily exposed to new attacks. The strongest arguments could fall away tomorrow. Religion must be able to emerge with authority, and that authority is not found in highly questionable evidences. Therefore, it must also conscientiously avoid all discussion with science and should not teach anything that would be disputable to it. It is nothing else than the sanction of the moral consciousness. Its only content is the recognition of our obligations as divine commands. Religion is morality. Whenever it understands this properly and does not go any further than it can and may according to its nature, it can further its own existence in peace and quiet.

Kantian philosophy is not a philosophy of little curled lines, of softly curved corners. It is might and majesty. Behind it, you sense a

---

Frederik van Eeden, *Little Johannes*, trans. Clara Bell (London: William Heinemann, 1895), 210–13.—Ed.

man. You hear a drumroll; you feel yourself called into a great moral struggle. You start to breathe again after all the attacks and objections with which the Enlightenment wanted to explain life and the world. I—a moral creature—do not simply have to stand aside and make way for all those reasonings of people who want to demonstrate that freedom and norms cannot exist. I may peacefully and trustingly remain believing what my heart's deepest intuition says to me: that I have to seek the good unconditionally.

Kant's ideas have not failed to exert great influence. Kant is a thinker who has yet to feel dated; yes, even in recent times he has come to the fore more strongly still. Standing in the middle of life, he did not try to cut life loose of all norms and laws but rather to ground those norms and laws in life itself. The Romantic movement that arose in that period and that risked glorifying the bad as long as it was great and mighty was more or less destroyed by Kant—or at least made to buckle. This thinker was so deeply marked by the exceptional value of the "moral law within me" [moralische Gesetz in mir] that he knew how to stand courageously against all skepticism.

Now when we consider this system more closely, we are immediately struck by the much deeper foundation that it possesses. It recognizes not only activity but also passivity. It is aware of the relative rightness of empiricism, accepts perception as a source of knowledge, but recognizes just as much the relative rightness of rationalism. It emphasizes the forms of viewing [Anschauung], space and time, and the forms of the intellect, the different categories. With this, it is sober enough to understand that these forms of thinking may not be considered innate ideas, as though the soul carries with it the concepts of causality, and so on, in a fully formed way, from its inception onward. It intuits that these forms are nothing more than aprioristic forms that first come to consciousness, to actuality, through contact with material provided by the senses. That is all far deeper and more mature than that which was provided by the earlier thinkers.

And not only this; Kant also intuited the limited right of human reason. He saw that we may not apply all manner of useful categories, which may reasonably be applied in particular areas, to wholly different terrains, where they do not in fact belong. He did not only perceive this, but he also elaborated it and tried to draw clean boundaries [between these terrains].

And finally, Kant gave right and worth to life, to personality. Other thinkers simply thought in a detached way [from life and personality] and did not care whether their conclusions might have been catastrophic for life itself. Kant understood that the heart has its own rights and that we must duly take this into account, all the more when the intellect does not emerge with its account. In his philosophy, you meet the human being; he intuits his responsibility and does not only want to theorize—he also wants to build up.

[Now] that is all very nice. Who would not gratefully receive it? Another question, though, is whether these thoughts make us ready to give a firm foundation to the personality or, indeed, if the personality has a right to this. That question is not so easily answered.

The great concepts of freedom, immortality, and God are [mere] postulates in Kant's philosophy. How do I come to have certainty regarding these concepts? By postulating them. I must believe in freedom because otherwise, life would be meaningless; because otherwise, the voice of conscience within me would be folly. I must believe in immortality because otherwise, my life would be meaningless. My life hardly even comes close to the ideal of the moral norm. It is only to be understood and valued as a fragment—in which case it is not so bad that I do not arrive at that norm in this life because this life is made complete in another life, after death. Why do I believe in God? Because otherwise, life would be meaningless. I would not have the least guarantee that my moral intuition is right that good leads to greater happiness and evil leads to punishment. Everything would be a confused and chaotic mess. It is only when I first see my obligation as a divine command and believingly trust that God sanctions that moral voice within me that it then becomes firm to me. In other words, God must exist, for otherwise, life would be meaningless and pointless. If God does not exist, there is no value in carrying on [with life] because it leads to nothing.

The meaninglessness of life is at stake in all these concepts. If I do not believe in it, then I cease to exist as a moral human being. But may I allow that tall building of concepts to rest on this threat to life itself? Do I not then receive the impression that these concepts are actually fictions that certainly do have [a degree of] practical necessity—because without them we could not live—but of which we cannot say very much more? They are founded on a psychological need: we need them, and therefore we create them. Otherwise, we do not become moral human beings. We must believe in them because otherwise, we would die. Life itself demands them with compelling force.

But this is exactly what the soul does *not* want. It does not want to create the existence of God, so to speak, because of moral necessity, so that God's existence would then do away with that moral necessity from the rear. The idea that we postulate [God's existence] because we need it in the struggle of life is itself [actually] equipped to remove the full power [of the ideas of God, immortality, and freedom]. I do not want to create for myself the ideas of freedom, of immortality, and of God because I need those concepts as a moral human being. The idea itself that I create them in order to move forward, to reach something, takes away the compelling power that is itself precisely the thing I need.

Stated differently still, each worldview is the attempt to conquer a worldvision, or at least to correct it and establish it on an objective basis. The worldvision is born of the personality and also makes the personality what it is—and yet a human being needs something more than this. He wants to test his worldvision; he wants an objective account of the existence of things in order to direct himself. The human being wants to form a worldview on the basis of objective considerations, and that will overcome his worldvision, and as such, that will elevate all his willing. If that is so, however, the center point of his worldview cannot lie in the will. [Otherwise,] the will would pull itself upward, and Kant—the strong, moral man—would doubtless seek a moral foundation that he thinks sufficient. But then, objectivity is not adequately established for this. First you say, "There *must* be freedom because otherwise, morality would be incomprehensible." Then, "Act morally because you are free!" First you say, "There must be a God because otherwise, there would be no moral order, and my moral intuition would find no adequate guarantee [i.e., that good leads to greater happiness, and evil, to judgment]." Then you follow this with: "Live morally because a God exists." The final practical conclusion never contains more than the starting presupposition. This is why it is never able to restrain the immoral impulses that lie within the human being.

All this is only in regard to the influence [of Kant's philosophy] on the personality. There are more questions, however, that merit a moment of our attention. It would be too great a diversion were we to try to look closely at the different ideas in Kant's epistemology one by one. In any case, the history of the last century traced out various elements [of it]. That having been said, we must indeed pause for a moment at the great contrast made by Kant between religion and philosophy. On the one hand, this contrast has as a consequence that religion can watch the philosophical duel as an independent party. The question, though, is whether such a relationship can be sustained. And then, it is immediately apparent that each religion that proceeds from the existence of God is drawn into philosophical discussion on all number of points, and that it cannot and may not possibly keep itself out of [that philosophical discussion]. From the outset, every person who believes in the existence of a God will have a different verdict on the questions of where all things came from, of the way things exist, of the goal for which the world does and must exist, on the questions of causality and teleology, creation and evolution, than the person who does not take these great ideas into account. This is so because [the person who believes in a God] weighs up different factors because he sees things in a different light. The whole of scientific-philosophical thought is dominated by it. Religion and science are not to be separated, and every violent attempt to do so must lead to great damage.

A third, and no less weighty, objection to Kantian thinking is this: that through him, far too strong an accent has been laid on human freedom. Doubtless, Kant was correct in protesting against the mechanical determinism that degraded the human being to a machine and thus that removed any responsibility from him. That determinism assumed that the laws of nature, the laws of causality, existed externally to the human being, automatically determined all his behavior, and, as such, took the soul out of the soul, the *I* out of the psychical processes. The moral revolution set in motion by this had to be powerfully broken because it was able to set a person [guilty of] the greatest sin at ease through the delusion that he could not have done anything different. Another question, however, is whether Kant posited his idea of freedom in the right way and laid it as the foundation for the rest of his considerations. Does the great "thou shalt" [*du sollst*] indeed always conclude in the "thou art able" [*du kannst*]? May we conclude the one from the other? Is the fulcrum that one gains in this way sufficiently warranted? Each of these questions leads to new difficulties. How must we then conceive of that freedom? Deeper consideration leads us to the result that recognizing the "thou shalt" [*du sollst*] in no sense contains or presupposes freedom and that the freedom from which Kant proceeds does not exist in that sense. There is no "thou art able" [*du kannst*] in the complete sense preached by Kant. To postulate this on the ground of moral norms is to take a leap that is itself neither valid nor true. Thus, the building that is Kantian practical philosophy does not stand on a firm foundation.

In the fourth place, and along with all this, the concept of God arrived at by Kant from his foundational idea is a dead and empty thing. It ends up outside all philosophical consideration. It serves only to give sanction to the moral norm. As such, it remains shadowy, idle; it has no flesh and blood. And neither can it because it is only a postulate. We can speak no further of it. It takes its leave behind all further consideration. It remains in the background of life, only giving support to the great "thou shalt" [*du sollst*]. It offers no rest, no comfort, no help, and no grace. It has neither color nor name. And it could not because in Kantian philosophy, belief in God has the moral intuition as its only fulcrum. That is the religious poverty of his system. And this poverty has clearly made its presence felt in the history of philosophy. You only need to consider the ideas of Fichte to see the views that inevitably came about from these Kantian foundations.

For Kant, though, it was not possible to think differently than he did, because he moved forward [on the belief that] the existence of God lay far beyond all experience. In essence, he was a deist. God is far away. God is absolutely out of reach. There is no divine voice that reaches the world.

If that is true, then the path he followed might indeed be the only path that a human being can [follow]. Then we would have to conclude, God is infinitely far off, unknowable [onkenbaar], but our thinking compels us toward him, and our moral intuition postulates his existence. That is then the only possible leap—the leap that we must take.

The question, though, is [precisely] whether that is true—whether that idea was not a wrong suggestion, through which the thinker Kant led the age of the Enlightenment down the wrong path. After all, in contrast to Kant, we hear the whispering of the mysticism of every age and people group, which confesses precisely the opposite: God is near to us; the quiet heart feels his presence. He is in our life. At every moment, we can trace a line from our life toward God.

And above that mysticism, the voice of the Christian faith resounds: God is near to us. He has spoken through prophets and apostles. He has spoken through and in Jesus Christ.

Mysticism and Revelation

UNTIL THIS POINT, we have discussed different worldviews that presented themselves to us as very concrete and real, that were creations of a particular time, and in which particular thinkers made their pronouncements. Now that we intend to deal with mysticism, [though,] we are entering a much more difficult terrain. Mysticism is a universal impulse that you will find everywhere and at all times. It is not bound to particular people and times, but rather, it fills the whole of history.

Turn your eye to ancient India, and in very early times you find a richly developed mystical life, of which the Vedic literature gives us a multifaceted image. The Upanishads brought these mystical tendencies to a richly developed state. Even in Buddhism, you can see all sorts of mystical moments without any difficulty. Through a number of its thinkers—namely, through Plato and Aristotle—Greece also developed ideas that proved to be fertile soil for mysticism. And we hardly have to recall the name of Neoplatonism, with its great representative Plotinus, to sense the sort of development that could come from these seeds. The mysteries of the more recent age, the heyday of the [Roman] Empire, bring us into contact with mystical movements that were wondrous, capricious, and Eastern in character but that have nonetheless wielded great influence. Even Islam, which in many regards [rests] on a deistic foundation, has given a place to mysticism and always holds within it a mixture of mystical movements. In Western Europe, mysticism knew an age of rich growth during the Middle Ages, the force of which has penetrated the modern age in all manner of ways. As such, everywhere in world history [*wereldgeschiedenis*], you will find mysticism as one of the mightiest currents to have moved human life.

If you were to ask me about the thinkers in the history of modern philosophy who are most marked by mystical tendencies, I would direct you to Spinoza before all others. Although his worldview is strongly rationalistic in structure, it has a mystical substrate in more than one regard. In more recent times, the philosophy of Schelling,[1] especially in his later period, brought mystical thoughts to further development. Different mystical tendencies were also at work in Schopenhauer,[2] as demonstrated by Dr. Hermann Wolf (*Personality and the Life of the Mind*).[3] And in the modern age, the mystical life has come into new bloom in all sorts of places. I only have to point out movements like theosophy, anthroposophy, Christian Science, and so on, to help you understand this. In art and literature, mysticism's influences are at work in many ways. Men such as Frederik van Eeden,[4] Maeterlinck,[5] Anker Larsen,[6] and many others have, as it were, brought mysticism into the public domain and spread it among the people. In his verses, Rainer Maria Rilke[7] has brought the beauty of this [philosophy] to an elevated expression. Mystical ideas and inclinations come to the surface in the plastic arts[8] and in painting (Toorop).[9] Our age, in its entirety, is overflowing with mystical influences.

Closely describing the character of mysticism is significantly more difficult than laying out its generalities. What should we actually un-

1   Friedrich Wilhelm Joseph von Schelling (1775–1854), the German Idealist philosopher.—Ed.
2   Arthur Schopenhauer (1788–1860), a German atheist philosopher.—Ed.
3   Hermann Wolf (1893–1942), a German-Dutch Jewish philosopher. Hermann Wolf, *Persoonlijkheid en geestesleven* (Haarlem: F. Bohn, 1927).—Ed.
4   Frederik van Eeden (1860–1932), a Dutch writer and psychiatrist who was influenced by Hinduism and Western mysticism.—Ed.
5   Maurice Maeterlinck (1862–1949), a Belgian playwright influenced by mysticism.—Ed.
6   Johannes Anker Larsen (1874–1957), a Danish actor and author.—Ed.
7   Rainer Maria Rilke (1875–1926), an Austrian poet and novelist.—Ed.
8   Plastic arts—arts that use preexisting materials (e.g., sculpture and ceramics).—Ed.
9   Jan Toorop (1858–1928), a Dutch-Indonesian painter.—Ed.

derstand by that word? Which movements may we understand by that
word? That is so difficult because we can never think of mysticism
separately from the various people who have emerged as its proponents.
The movement takes on a distinct character according to the countries,
the eras, the circumstances in which it has arisen. In fact, it is actually
"impossible to grasp and to sketch mysticism as such. It never emerges
in a vacuum but rather in connection with religion and culture. And not
only in general. It always binds itself to a particular form or grouping
of forms that is cultural or religious in nature."[10] This is why whenever
someone tries to describe the essence of mysticism, he quickly runs the
risk of sketching a particular type (which he treats as normal) without
noticing that you fail to do justice to so many other types and forms that
were just as significant. We find a typical example of this in the otherwise
excellent *Psychology of Worldviews* by Karl Jaspers.[11] Jaspers describes
the "crucial feature" [*entscheidende Merkmal*] of the "mystical mindset"
[*mystische Einstelling*] as "the rejection of the confrontation of subject
and object (of *I* and the object). Therefore, all that is mystical is never
to be understood as content but only as experience, which is to say, to
define the real meaning subjectively and without reason."[12] This observation is doubtless a fair characterization of various forms of mysticism
but does not do justice to other equally essential currents [within it].

This seems to be the case as soon as you try to form a concept of
mysticism. As a general trait, you might say that [people] act mystically
[in search of] union with God, that it is "striving for complete union
with God" [*Streben nach der vollkommenen Vereinigung mit Gott*].[13] But

---

10 W. J. Aalders, *Mystiek: Haar vormen, wezen, waarde* (Groningen: J. B. Wolters, 1928), 298.
    [The original Dutch reads, . . . *onmogelijk de mystiek als zoodanig, zonder meer te grijpen
    en te teekenen. Zij komt nooit en nergens zuiver voor, maar altijd in verband met godsdienst
    en cultuur. En niet alleen in het algemeen. Zij verbindt zich altijd met een bepaalden vorm
    of vormenverbinding van cultureelen of godsdienstigen aard.*—Ed.]
11 Karl Jaspers (1883–1969), a German philosopher and political theorist.—Ed.
12 The original German reads, . . . *die Aufhebung des Gegenüberstehens von Subject und
    Objekt (von Ich und Gegenstand). Daher ist alles Mystische nie als Inhalt, sondern nur
    als Erlebnis, d.h. subjektiv und ohne den eigentlichen, nu rim Erlebnis ergreif baren Sinn
    rational zu bestimmen.*—Ed.
13 J. Zahn, *Einführung in die Christliche Mystik* (Paderborn: Schöningh, 1922), s. 34.

this definition allows for a range of possibilities that immediately spring into existence in various forms. How should one conceive of that union? Should one think of it as an absolute "becoming one" with divinity, so that one's own existence is given up? Is it then not to be seen as becoming conscious of the unity with God that in actual fact already exists? The human being as a part of, a moment in, God? A tiny wave in the ocean of divinity? It is also possible, however, that one conceives of that union as a form of fellowship in which the human being continues to exist as an individual, as a human being, but, as it were, meets divinity, comes into contact with divinity. Does one deem that union already possible in this life, or does one think that it can be actualized here only in very shadowy, patchy ways and that it can be acquired only in the full sense in the hereafter, in the next world [*Jenseits*]? Which other functions [of the soul] are emphasized in this union? Does one regard that union with God exclusively as a matter of knowing [*kennen*], as a viewing of God, a *visio Dei*? Or does one situate the center point in feeling, in the heart, in the *fruitio Dei*, the enjoyment of God, in being blessed by God? Mostly, these moments emerge together; they cannot be thought of without one another. Mysticism seeks "the pure truth and the sweetness of God in equal measure."[14] Nonetheless, the accent can be utterly different. And as well as this, how does one conceive of that union? Is it absolute rest, an entrance into complete silence? Or must we consider that union precisely as an impulse toward activity, toward serving God, toward life and activity? You see that the simple description of the search for union with God makes a mixture of forms and ideas difficult. And precisely in that elaboration, we find ourselves standing again before the great questions of worldview. There it is the worldviews that define the answer, that will push one person in this direction and another person in another direction.

Thus, when someone thinks he can develop a conclusive and well-rounded image of mysticism, without taking a long list of nuances into

---

14 Aalders, *Mystiek*, 318. [The original Dutch reads, *evenzeer de zuivere waarheid als de zoetheid van God*.—Ed.]

account, he goes wrong. It is exactly these characteristic distinctions that often set the different currents within mysticism directly against one another and that must lead to great contrasts. Namely, these are the more or less pantheistically flavored mystical systems, which must be distinguished from all Christian mysticism with great care and a clear emphasis. Mysticism is not a single worldview. Rather, it only emerges in relation to different worldviews, and as such, it has a wholly different character.

When we put it in those terms, we do not make it easy for ourselves to give a sketch of the mystical currents in their connection to personality and worldview. In a few short words, we will first try to provide a schema for the more pantheistically tinted mysticism, which is more or less isolated from the great religions, in order, therefore, to determine its relationship to Christianity succinctly. Our first overview must be a fairly general one. It cannot possibly get deeply into particularities and also runs the risk of elaborating one particular form of mystical life too much. And yet, for the sake of clarity, we must provide one such brief characterization.

Mysticism in general, and thus also non-Christian mysticism, assumes that God is near to us. God is not infinitely far off, such that we cannot know or approach him in any way. Rather, he is in us and with us. All mysticism rests on the idea of the immanence of God, God's indwelling of the human being. Although Christian mysticism—which we will later see—always draws a sharp boundary between God and the human being, as a rule that [boundary] is more or less vague and unclear in non-Christian [mysticism]. It also assumes that the human being possesses an organ with which it can mentally [*ervaren*] and physically [*beleven*] experience and know [*kennen*] God's presence. Naturally, that organ is not the eye because the eye only brings us into contact with the sensible world. It is also no more the intellect or even reason, which certainly can think and give meaning about God but which is powerless in feeling his presence. There is, however, a different organ, the mind's eye, the heart, which feels God (here in the sense of "is aware of"), that senses his nearness, that is able to provide contact with him. It is extremely difficult to indicate in more detail what is to be understood by that organ and what worth should be attached to it. It makes us think of a "seeing," but it is not bodily, not sensory. It is a spiritual seeing, a becoming filled, a becoming warmed by the nearness of that Most High Being.

Mysticism chases after that union. It goes without saying that this seeing of God cannot always take place without some preparation. The spiritual eye must be exercised and all those disturbing forces carefully pushed out of view. For the most part, this preparation consists in asceticism, in fasting, in all sorts of exercises, in setting oneself apart. It often includes [the idea] that a person must withdraw from the busyness of life, from the maelstrom of daily events, and give himself over to solitude, to a great and deep silence. The eye can see God only when it holds all other noises far away from itself. The silence that can then come on the soul is not an unconsciousness, even though it can sometimes look like that. It is a different [way of] directing the powers of the soul, a lifting up of the self [to move] above the sensible to the eternal. With this [pursuit of transformation], quiet meditation—silent, deep thought about eternal things—must often smooth the path and bring [that person's] soul into the right mood. Naturally, this meditation is to do with contemplation, in lifting up the self toward God himself, in approaching him. Among many Eastern peoples, entirely different paths are often taken. There, through all sorts of different means—dance, monotonal music, the endless repetition of certain incantations—people try to bring themselves into an ecstatic state, which then makes fellowship with God possible. In a certain sense, the fellowship itself—the mystical ecstasy—suddenly comes on that person. It is given to him, and even though he has prepared himself, that person feels that he is passive, receptive. It is a wondrous moment in which every sensory need stands still, in which every inclination and thought is wiped out and the soul experiences nothing but the unspeakable greatness and majesty of God.

For this reason, it is always very difficult to express what is experienced in such a moment. For many great mystics, it was always such that they were brought into a sort of unconsciousness by this all-powerful emotion. Sometimes they could spend hours in such a state of ecstasy, but during those hours they were completely cut off from the world of sensation. Even when they were beaten or bitten or otherwise tormented in such a time, they did not notice. Mystical ecstasy is so overwhelming that every other sensation is dwarfed by it. Insofar as the mystics were then able to give an account of what they had seen, they mostly made use of symbolic expressions. Now some of them emphasized that they had seen the divine as an incomprehensibly glorious light. Then again, they expressed it as having seen God as the most essential, the very highest Being; that they had now experienced for the first time that every other being is a shadow, an image from a dream, and that God alone must be known as the substance, as the absolute Being. If you keep on asking [about the divine], then mostly you receive the answer that it is [a reality] that is hard to describe differently. The divine is completely without form, timeless, without essence. He is a dark abyss into which the soul sinks but of whom it can later give no more description. [The soul] could not say, "It was like this or that." It could provide no description of the divine. Everything it could say was most negative: the divine does not fit in a single concept; it transcends everything; it is an unutterable glory.

In particular, though, the emphasis often falls on the being of God, in distinction to nonbeing. God is the complete one, and when the soul comes into contact with him, everything else fades away. Having withdrawn from ecstasy, a person sees the world as an illusion, as something unreal. Even our own existence is no longer certain; one feels that one no longer actually *is*, that only God *is*, and that the human being only *is* insofar as he is one with God. In particular, sensory impressions lose their worth and meaning. The material world is now nothing, is an enchantment, a delusion, a veil. One must step out of that delusion and approach God as the only existing one. Fellowship with God elevates the soul immeasurably far, turns the human being himself into a little divine flame, and at the same time extinguishes all the chasing after sensory satisfaction within him.

But for the rest, God's being remains entirely undefined. Mystical literature often emphasizes that God is formless divinity, that he is unknowable depth. We can say nothing about him, because all that we say is a limitation that falls short of his absoluteness. He is not assimilated or apprehended by the soul. We receive no clear and well-rounded image of him. We remain foreign and childish in our distance. God is utterly other. Every word about him is a lie, a betrayal of his majesty. He cannot be known [*gekend*] but only experienced, gazed on. And that experience does not lead to a clear and definite concept because he exceeds each concept and can be spoken of in no single concept.

All these ideas bring with them a certain attitude to life. As a rule, the morality of this mysticism is that one must seek a life that is free of the self—a life that once and for all gives up the folly that you would be something next to or alongside God and that finds its highest fulfillment in pure passivity. You must free yourself of all love and hate, of all the heart's passions and desires, of all honor and repute, and in the attentive silence of solitude, you must direct yourself wholly and only toward the only God. It is only the attentive life that does not think and act and see itself, that makes [a person] see and know him and be filled by him. Life's only morality, then, is world flight, withdrawing yourself from every sphere of life. Every impulse means that God is pushed further from view and that one loses sight of him. Such a life has little by way of meaning or goal. The only goal that it allows is that of more or less freeing yourself from delusion, from idleness, and climbing ever higher toward the true nearness of God. No effort to conquer the world was ever born of such a movement. Rather, it strikes all love for the world dead. Life dissolves into a groping after eternity and a turning away from time.

A worldview is tightly bound to this morality for life. The brilliant shine [that you see on] things is a hindrance. You must penetrate to that which is inward and approach the eternal Being behind that appearance. The world itself is a blinding of the soul. Therefore, this mysticism is always more or less idealistic in flavor.

And thus, you see a few traits of the common, pantheistically tinted mysticism. You will come across varieties of this in their clearest form in Indian philosophy, which has subjected itself with exceptional might to these idle abstractions. There, by the way, to the present day, the mystical life is earnestly pursued in all its fullness. Some of these ideas, however, also strayed into the Christian mysticism of the Middle Ages. They do not belong there because they are essentially of pagan extraction. Nonetheless, they were brought into the West from the Neoplatonism of Pseudo-Dionysius the Areopagite.[15] There they intermingled with all sorts of Christian ideas and currents.

Now, that mysticism undoubtedly contains much that is beautiful and worthy. It sees God as no mere idea that one affirms or denies on the basis of all sorts of arguments but as a reality that one experiences, that one can behold in a certain sense. This is why this direction is always so very alluring to all those of a deeper nature. In it, as it were, they feel themselves plucked out of the multiplicity and bitterness of earthly cares and worries and taken up into another world that warms and enriches them inwardly. The pessimism that undergirds this mysticism also contains something attractive. It does not laugh off the misery of life. Rather, it groans under it. But it then points to a way of escape in the inner chambers of the soul, where the light of eternity can penetrate. The praise for silence voiced in many tones by this mysticism is also ultimately one of the special traits loved by many. Away from all the noise and heaviness of earthly life, it shows us the great treasures of a quiet, listening life. The most elevated activity that a human being can develop is that he listens to the voice of that hidden world that softly pulses through us. "With silence, let us honor the mystery that is above!"[16]

And yet, despite all that is worthy [in this], it is not difficult to demonstrate the poverty of this mysticism. In the first place, this regards its ideas about God. God is impassive peace, eternal stillness. The human being seeks him, but he does not seek the human being. He is

---

15 Pseudo-Dionysius the Areopagite, a Greek Neoplatonist and theologian in the late fifth to early sixth century.—Ed.

16 For this reference from Pseudo-Dionysius, see Ben Schomakers, *Over mystieke theologie* (Kampen: Kok Agora, 1990), 3.—Ed.

airy, elusive. He evades all description. He has evaporated into a haze, a twilight. He is sometimes called a light because approaching him is to approach pure glory, but he is also often called darkness because he withdraws himself from all being known [*kennen*]. Ultimately, you cannot pray to this God. There is no comfort in him, no help, no salvation. One can only worship him in deep devotion.

The same applies with regard to life. This particular mysticism gives us no support in life, no guiding principle. It draws us out of life; it cuts us loose from love and from all seeking and striving. It forces and compels us in its great silence. The virtues of life—like love, faithfulness, surrender, bravery, self-sacrifice, and so many more—are neither taught nor supported by this mysticism. It sucks us out of life and loosens our connections to the world and life. This is why it is so unsatisfactory in terms of morality. In the struggle of life, it leaves us alone with our distress and temptation. It sheds no light on our existence and gives no goal or ideal to our works. It leaves the poverty of our life untouched. It does all this more or less intentionally. It is hostile to the world [*weltfeindlich*]. It wants to cut the human being loose from the world. Its highest ideal remains Nirvana, "the blowing out."[17] It brings all the abilities and gifts of life into a completely different direction and puts the will to death. For this reason, this mysticism has never been held by many. It bears an aristocratic character. It chooses its servants from few circles. It does not stimulate peoples and gives no happiness or norms to a life in all its tumults. It does not reconcile the human being to God or the world.

The same mysticism, however, that we have now seen in a more or less isolated form takes on an entirely different character when we find it connected to Christianity. Christianity is also a religion that believes in the nearness of God, that assumes the immanence of God, that emphasizes fellowship between God and the human being. Christianity also speaks of becoming one with God, a becoming one not in

---

17 In Indian religions, the Sanskrit term *nirvana* ("the blowing out," in the sense of a flame being extinguished) refers to a state of perfect stillness, in which one attains the highest happiness and liberation from all attachment to the world.—Ed.

the sense of sinking into the abyss of divinity but in the sense of moral, spiritual fellowship, as a gift, full of rich promises.

In Christianity, all these ideas receive entirely different content through its worldview, which is wholly differently focused. The Christian religion draws every line differently because it sees and preaches God and the world, life and death, norms and sin, differently. As such, all Christian mysticism, despite this history, has a totally different structure and build.

This is already evident in that it brings to the fore, with such tremendous emphasis, that God is a God who speaks. The first page of the Bible tells of God "speaking." He is the stillness of absolute being but at the same time life, power, the absolute will. Augustine portrays him as being, consciousness, and will. He is the one from whom an overwhelming power proceeds, who speaks and acts.

That speaking is speech in a thousand forms. It comes to us through the majestic glory of nature, in the roar of spring and the rattle of thunder, in the bubbling brook, and in the unending loneliness of the desert. It comes to us in the course of life, in the paths of history, in the voice of the conscience. That is all universal. As such it speaks to every human being. But there is also another speech that bears a very particular character. Pious, old Abraham heard this in moments of God being incomprehensibly close when he said, "I am God, the Almighty One." Moses, the leader of the pilgrim people, knew it as such when [God] called himself, "I will be who I will be." That wondrous speech did not happen often. For very long periods, it was scarce and poor. But those who had heard it kept it like a great secret in the depths of their hearts. It was the word, the word of him whom their souls had sought. And that word grew. Over the centuries it became richer and fuller. It was often wrathful speech about sin and falling away, but it was also speech of inner comfort, of deep compassion, of grace and promise.

At the end [of this speech] stands Jesus Christ. He is the Word who says who God is and how we must know [kennen] him. The disciples who were around him understood this. When they heard his words, it was as though they had heard God himself. When he pronounced a verdict on someone, there was a voice deep in their souls that said to them that this was not an accidental expression of sympathy or antipathy but that such a person had been judged by God. When they heard him, they knew that they had been lifted above all the affairs and wavering of this world and that they stood before the face of the Almighty. For this reason, they called him the Word, in whom God expresses within the world who he is. And he himself confirms this: "Whoever has seen me has seen the Father" [John 14:9]. The disciples could not describe what it was deep within them that made them think this [about him], but there was a power that drove them toward him, and that made them say, "You have the words of eternal life!" [John 6:68]. That was God's great speech; that was the reflection of his light; that was the Word.

And all that speaking is self-referential, is a revealing, a speaking out of who God is. In God, there is life and love and volition and power. [This was] not always a speaking in words. Often it also came in promptings, in miracles, in great deeds, but it was always the case that the eternal spoke to the human being.

On that basis, the [Christian] religion expanded much more richly and fully than was ever possible in mysticism. The key issue in this was faith. Faith is something wholly different from mystical experience. With mysticism that is isolated from all revelation, it was always the case that as long as a human being lived in a rich mystical vision, he felt rich, but as soon as that was taken from him, he collapsed into the misery of deep abandonment. He had nothing left; the light had left him; he did not have one memory that would inspire him. In Christianity, that is different. There the human being has the word as an imperishable treasure that speaks to him of God—also in moments when he himself is alone and abandoned. It might seem to him that God is not merciful or almighty, that all life's experiences mislead him. And yet he stands with the word in his hands. And despite this [impression of abandonment], "This is what he is like! I believe!" By faith, the human being stands above all experiences. Often he can go against the appearance of things and cling to God.

That faith is an extremely tender and wondrous thing. How is it that a person hears the word and immediately knows [*weet*] with incomprehensible certainty, "This is what God is like!"; that deep within him there is something that gives a firm connection to that word; that he no longer doubts but knows [*weet*]? [How is it] that the human being stands before Jesus and senses with the same firmness, "You are the Son of the living God"? That faith is not a recognizing by the intellect, although the intellect also has a part in it. That faith is not a feeling and experiencing by the heart, although the heart also works in it. That faith is a thing from the whole person, from all his powers and gifts. [It is something] he does with the whole of his soul. And yet that is not to say everything of it. In faith, there is something that exceeds the person. In faith, there is a voice from God within him that binds him to the word of God, which is external to him: "Flesh and blood has not revealed this to you, but my Father who is in heaven" [Matt. 16:17]. It is the deeply hidden speaking, the whispering of God in the soul that binds the soul to God and that makes God known in the word that it speaks. Then the soul is bound to God on every side, and it enjoys being surrounded by the fellowship of God. The light must break into his heart to discover him in the light: "In your light do we see light!" [Ps. 36:9].

This is why mystical experience has a wholly different character in Christianity. It is not a great ecstasy, a treading into the dark abyss. It is an inner fellowship with God in the word, a life with God through the word. That word can then be thought of in the broadest sense. His word is in forests and in seas. But his Word is especially in Jesus Christ. In him we see the Father himself; he is the revelation of the Father in the world. If there are days when the soul feels itself further from God, when [the soul] becomes inwardly cold and dull, it still has the word that gives direction to its life and that it can expect and hope in. In Christianity, interaction with God is thought of as mediated by Jesus as the prophet, as the Word, of God.

That interaction is possible for us through and offered to us in Holy Scripture. That book describes and provides us with that whole and full revelation of God. The more often and the more deeply we investigate and search the Bible, we always find greater treasures from God. The riches that have come forth from that book are incomprehensible. You need to spend your entire life wandering through it, from day to day, to understand something of the glorious gift that God has given us in it. It gives light to our life, comfort to our pain; confronts us over our sin; offers us grace when we are bowed down; makes us happy and thankful, humble and childlike; and finally—because it has unlocked the mysteries of the ages for us—it makes us see death without alarm.

A second idea that gives [mysticism] a completely different character within Christianity is that of guilt. Pagan mysticism leaps easily over the abyss from the finite to the infinite, from the sinful human being to the Holy God. Unity [between them] is found and experienced easily—it even becomes an identity. Christianity casts these things in a completely different light. In numerous images, it portrays the astonishing distance between God and the human being. It paints the distance in natural terms because the human, as "dust and ashes" [Gen. 18:27], contrasts with the eternal [God]. It paints the distance particularly in moral terms, through which the human discovers his guilt and contrast with the Holy God. That distance is expressed in all manner of ways. Symbolically, we find it illustrated in the double curtain that kept the Holy of Holies in the temple from the view of the people and in the sacrifices that were necessary before the priest could enter the Holy Place. Through all those symbols, you find the idea of distance. God is hidden from the sinful human being. Fellowship with him is actually impossible.

Well, it is indeed possible but only by way of reconciliation. First, relationship with God must be restored, the human being must be reconciled, before there can be fellowship. That reconciliation is given to us in Christ as priest. Brokenness of heart and smallness of soul are necessary to receive the great treasure of forgiveness, in faith, from the hand of him who reconciles us to God. It is only after this, through this, that fellowship is possible. The outpouring of the Spirit follows the Easter celebration of the resurrection. Fellowship can come only when the great guilt-distance is taken away. And thus, that fellowship is mediated in him, the great priest of reconciliation.

That fellowship that is given in the outpouring of the Spirit, on the grounds of reconciliation, is a costly gift. The Bible is able to illustrate this fellowship of the Spirit in the most intimate and deep way. He always dwells within us; he is the quiet compulsion to prayer; we are his temple; he makes our will bend, gifts us with inner warmth and joy; he makes us grow in faith, makes us peaceful in adversity—in short, it is from fellowship with him that the whole of our life is inwardly renewed. All these workings [of the Spirit] are so tender and wondrous that they often entirely evade [our] reflection. Nonetheless, the human being can certainly experience their power. There are days when he notices the nearness of the Spirit as very real, when he knows [*weet*], in the deepest sense of the word, what it is to be "near unto God." In that fellowship, there is blessedness, emotion, great inner happiness that cannot be described and that far exceeds every other happiness.

In the third place, Christianity places this in the foreground: complete fellowship, the contemplation of God, is possible only when the last spores of the stain of impurity are removed from the heart, when holiness has entered life and Christ rules the soul as King. Only then can a person find that fellowship in all its fullness. The very highest fellowship is not given in this life, even though a glimpse of it can pulse through the heart from time to time. It belongs, rather, to the kingdom that is to come. The gospel tells us little about this, but what it does tell us of it is strikingly sober: "We shall see face to face" [1 Cor. 13:12 NIV].

From all this, it seems that mysticism in Christianity is governed by completely different ideas. It does not leap over deep chasms. It has means. It is mediated by Jesus Christ as prophet, priest, and king. It is a mysticism of distance, as opposed to the mysticism of identity known in the pagan world. This makes it no less inward, no less warm, but certainly much less easy. It demands that we are humbled by our sense of sin and our belief in grace, it demands that we sense our lostness in order that we allow ourselves to be found.

When we think more and more about these things, it immediately seems to us that an entirely new worldview is offered to us in Christianity. This is easily shown in a few points.

In the first place, Christianity denies the possibility—whether that be through empiricism, whether that be through reason, or any other way—of gaining insight into the deepest parts of the truth. This is because our perceiving and our thinking are no longer pure or pristine. In all his thinking and knowing [*kennen*], the human being is darkened through the power of the evil that holds his soul captive. He cannot approach the questions of life and world unprejudiced, and because his personality is not integrated, his worldview cannot be true. The truth is not only an intellectual good; it is also a moral good. The great thing that can lift a person across the chasm of his sinful prejudices is faith in him who speaks and in his word. That faith itself is a miracle; it rests in God's witness in the human heart. It is not dry, not calculating; it is just as active as it is passive; it is divine in its origin and content. With this, we do not say that all empiricism and all thinking must always be fruitless, but we do say that the sinful human being cannot arrive at *the* worldview [and cannot arrive] at *the* truth. On limited terrain, in all sorts of areas of science, the human being can think things that are beautiful and true, but when he approaches *the* final questions of thought and life, his soul's compass always proves defective because he does not want God, because he is at enmity with God. The worldview that can lift our life upward cannot be born of ourselves, must be thought of by God, must be given to us, must be spoken to us. In Christianity, that is not simply an incidental element. Rather, it is the keystone on which everything rests.

In the second place, it is notable that Christianity takes an idiosyncratic stance with regard to all the questions of worldview. We can summarize it in a paradox: on the one hand, it sees the boundary of pantheism, which regards the immanence and indwelling of God as the mystery of the world [*wereldgeheim*], and on the other hand, it sees the boundary of deism, which places God immeasurably far away in the idea of transcendence. Christianity points both of them—

one just as much as the other—back to, and establishes the truth in, the union of both. In the same way, it sees itself as hemmed in by determinism, which considers all life to be determined by unchangeable laws, and the indeterminism that far too strongly emphasizes the concept of freedom against it. [Christianity] sets bondage and freedom, divine order and human responsibility, alongside one another. In the same way, it binds and reconciles heteronomy and autonomy. We do not create our own laws but are subject to the law of God. On the other side, the law of God does not land on our lives from beyond and above because God writes it in our hearts. It is our conscience itself that bears witness to it. It receives the reality of mind and matter, and as such, it denies materialism and idealism. It recognizes activity and passivity, causality and teleology. It maintains the distinctiveness of the organic over against the mechanical and of the animate over against the inanimate. It recognizes the reality of the empirical and of reason and honors the rights of intellect and heart. It remains on guard against pessimism and optimism and sees both progress and regress in history. It sees life as summarized in sadness and joy; it confesses righteousness and grace, punishment and forgiveness. In every line that it draws, there is always a kink, always a bulge in the middle. It never approaches history from a single concept, never fails to do justice to what happens by forcing it into a straitjacket of one-sidedness. It makes no attempt to explain life and the world from one single, all-dominating idea. From a philosophical perspective, that may be the problem with Christianity, but through it, it has that breadth of vision toward life and the world that elevates the human being. It recognizes the different spheres, the different terrains of things that happen in their distinctiveness. It does no damage to the individual in relation to the crowd or to the whole in relation to the parts. It peers into the world with a breadth and roominess that can indeed be painful for our thinking but that creates space for love, for paying attention to each thing in its particularity. And finally, it is also brave enough to recognize that we do not yet see the reconciliation of the many apparent contradictions but that we must believingly await that we will indeed eventually see it, when the fracture in our own soul itself will be taken away.

It goes along with all this that the gospel sees the relationship of the human being to God as a lively, a moral relationship. Non-Christian mysticism conceived of that relationship completely differently. It saw the seeking person [as one] who thirsts for and approaches God as the eternal stillness. There all the tension, all the seeking, lay on the side of the human being, and all the rest lay on the side of God. The gospel puts forward that relationship as much more multiform, much richer, and thus more difficult, as a concept. It portrays the human being as a God abandoner who deviates, who flees, who fears—who in all his life breaks his connection to God through sin and weakness. And in contrast to this, in fine detail, Jesus portrays the shepherd who seeks, the God who reaches out for the fallen human being. Through this, its view of God becomes very different, and proper justice is done to the love of God, who seeks and finds. The person of Jesus Christ himself is the greatest proof, the greatest gift of God's love. In that love, there is holiness, such a holiness that it does not tolerate but rather consumes the evil in the human being. In that love, there is reconciliation, grace, comfort, mercy. It softens the heart and makes [you] flee to the merciful one. It makes you fear the holy wrath [of God] and long for complete forgiveness. It awakens that strange longing within the human being, that desire to be changed, that desire to live out of that overwhelming gratitude for the love of God. It elevates a person's highest powers. And in all that, it is always God himself who does this in the human being through his Spirit, who makes him into a new man. The gospel has no words that are great and full enough to explain the infinite fullness of the love of God in Jesus Christ, but it awakens that faith in the heart, that mighty emotion of letting yourself be grasped by the hand of the eternal one.

When you step into the gospel from the sterile deadness of many mystical systems, it always strikes you afresh that the gospel awakens a richly variegated relationship with God in life. It makes every one of the heart's strings vibrate: humility and confession of sin, endless trust, love, thankfulness, a powerful desire to be converted, an ideal in life, vocation, an irrepressible longing for the future vision of God, silence, and devotion. The mysticism that springs up from this is lively from the outset. This is so because God himself, as the gospel reveals him, is living. How often the call to the living God resounds in the Bible: "My soul thirsts for God, / for the living God" [Ps. 42:2]. Jesus is the revelation of that living God: he is "the Son of the living God" [Matt. 16:16].

It is not easy to stand on the heights of the gospel. Those who peer into Christianity often feel themselves deeply disappointed. The royal freedom of the Christian person is often crumpled up into a *petit bourgeois* politeness. Saying yes to the Word by faith, having been deeply touched by God's Spirit, is often flattened into an intellectual, dry, and cold confession. Often, it is as though the bare walls are still standing, but all life, all light, all warmth has been banished, as though there is no more talk of interaction with God. The animating, love-awaking power of the gospel often seems to have lost its effect in the heart. Often, we carry this treasure in jars of clay. Before all else, everyone who bemoans this might keep a close eye on his own life. He might recognize that it is also so for himself, that he himself is poor and flat. The greatness of the Word—who came to us from eternity—shines high above our lives.

The highest mystical expression of the Christian life is prayer. That prayer is fellowship, interaction [with God]. It is not an ecstatic [experience]. Rather, it is a voyage from darkness toward the light. It is a combining of all the powers of the soul and a directing of them toward God. It is a seeking of his face, an allowing of the voice of God to speak within you. It is an asking and a confessing, a thanking and a praising. Sometimes it is only a standing before the eternal one in his infinite majesty and a humble recognition that simply says, "God!" Then [that prayer] is immersed in the worship of God; it has no words, no language. Then it moves toward the seeing of God. Then it is as though the soul sees something of him from afar, and through that glimpse alone you are moved to the core. And then that great homesickness for him is awakened [within you]: "When shall I come and appear before God?" [Ps. 42:2]. The heart that has been pushed down into the darkness of sin and despair waits and longs for the great tomorrow, when he will be all in all [1 Cor. 15:28].

Personality and Worldview

NOW THAT WE HAVE MADE FORAYS into different parts of the great mass of worldviews, we must return to the questions from which we first set out and thus try to summarize our conclusion. As we do so, we can place a few remarks in the foreground. In our investigation, we have not tried to provide a schematization of all possible worldviews. In fact, we did not want to try this. It is possible to place different "mindsets" [Einstellungen] alongside each other in order to compare different types of worldview. It is not possible, though, to deal with their fullness exhaustively. Human life and thought is ultimately so rich and nuanced that it does not fit within a particular window.

That already seems to be the case when you test it using a single word. We have the pantheistic worldview. In pantheism there are indeed a few great ideas that can be formulated more closely. It proceeds from the identity of God and world, from the individual I with the "world soul" [Wereldziel], from the atman and Brahma. Doubtless, this [description] contains a variety of very weighty consequences. Nonetheless, when someone intends to sketch out a worldview from this [summary], he makes a gross mistake—because within pantheism there are so many possibilities, so many further nuances that you soon notice that the word *pantheism* is one word that summarizes a whole group of worldviews that deserve to be more closely defined with a range of adjectives. You have idealistically inclined pantheism, which summarizes the world as an appearance, as a mirage, and which sees the spirit as the only thing that is true. You have naturalistic pantheism, that (here and there) comes very close to materialism, that barely makes room for norms and higher spiritual values. You meet Spinozan pantheism, which believes in a deeper identity of matter and spirit, which it summarizes as attributes of one infinite substance. You will get to deal with mystical pantheism, which sees God especially as the deepest essence of all things. Then you will quickly experience how pantheism can join itself to optimistic evolutionism but is also very often paired with the very deepest pessimism; pantheism can be the foundation of socialism but can just as easily lead to individualism *par excellence.* In short, [you will see] that something is indeed said with that one word, but [what is said] is relatively so thin that you must approach the concept closely from every side if you want to gain a reasonably clear and concrete image of it. That is what makes each classification of worldviews so difficult. You must proceed through numerous precise subdivisions. You always see new forms emerge. You must collapse the diversity into a few dominant types, or you quickly become reserved [in how you speak] among the swelling possibilities.

Now, we have been scrupulous in avoiding all that. Indeed, this was not what we did in our investigation. We only wanted to sketch a few of the worldviews most prominent in the modern age and demonstrate that these worldviews were of the utmost significance for the life of the personality. They are born of the personality but also have an effect on the personality. They are forces that can move and lead the whole life of the personality.

With this, in the second place, we must focus our attention on the phenomenon by which the most philosophically reasoned worldviews only ever become the possession of a tiny number of minds and only trickle down to the general public very weakly indeed. When you go among the ordinary people to investigate what sort of worldview resides there, you would perhaps be disappointed by the discovery that all the digging and searching of the greatest minds was unable to give a firm guideline to the people. People live and act as though there is actually no worldview, as though you never actually have to deal with the questions [of God, life, and the world]. Most worldviews are appropriated only by the intellectual aristocracy. The people in general know the foundational principles of materialism, feel a power within it that they cannot ignore, but they are blind to the deeper considerations of Spinoza and Kant. That feels like ivory-tower philosophizing, which is irrelevant to the people. Only a few individuals are moved by great systems of thought.

On the other hand, though, you will find with deeper considerations that the different worldviews we have discussed can indeed be found in "seed form" [*keimartig*] among the people. This can easily be illustrated with a few examples. For instance, the man who emphatically assures you, "Stay away from me with all your nonsense about God and the soul. I only believe in what I can see!" is in principle an empiricist and, as such, is a naive empiricist. If he were to think consistently, he would undoubtedly become an empiricist [by name], and if he then thought even more consistently, he would perhaps simultaneously be healed [of his empiricism]. Naturally, though, he never progresses that far. The mentality [*Einstellung*], however, is present within him. Another person would respond to you, "I do not know what I must think of all these things, but the only thing I feel, when I go out walking on a summer's evening, is that there is a God, a silent, secretive power in nature all around me!" Often without even knowing it, [that person] is a mystic. The mystical mentality [*Einstellung*] has taken hold of him. He is far too inconsistent and does not think through things enough, but the seed is present. A third person will perhaps say to you, "Life is much too busy to waste your time on all that nonsense; I do not believe we will ever understand things properly, but I think you must live a good life, must listen to your conscience, and must try to be as good [a person] as possible!" While he does not know it and has not thought about it, he more or less stands with Kant. If he would think consistently, he would feel and notice that. In other words, the different worldviews that we have met are present as mentalities [*Einstellungen*] within the different people we interact with every day. In a certain sense, they are far more common than we perhaps would superficially believe. The task of these thinkers was to work out the unconscious presuppositions of life, to think consistently, and thus also to make plain their consequences.

Of all the worldviews that we have discussed here, in our Western world there are only two that have the ability to become commonplace among the masses—that live among people not only as mentalities [*Einstellungen*] but as worldviews. These two are atheistic materialism and positive Christianity. No one, it seems, accepts the first of these unreservedly. Even the most consistent practical materialist still feels all sorts of reservations in his heart. When hearing spiritual stories, for example, or other miraculous phenomena, he will always experience something of the idea that many things are true that have not been understood, about which he has no idea. In numerous things, he will demonstrate a striking superstition, believing that thirteen is an unlucky number, that Friday is an unlucky day, and so on. Alongside this, he will be inclined, more or less, to view the way his life goes as an intentional plan. In days of adversity, he will have the feeling that this is always how it will go for him. He will think, "Just when I want to go out, it *obviously* starts raining." That one word, *obviously*, points out that he is not as atheistic as he believes he is. He feels deeply that a higher power governs life, but his confession of faith regarding that power contains no other doctrine than this: "God is behind all things to torment you, to work against you deliberately." This is the inner reservation that he has always held against materialism, although this reservation does not contain much power. In the daily practice of his life, he is still a materialist. For him, that materialism means as much as the denial of all absolute norms and of life having a destiny. For the vast majority of our population, the struggle of worldviews is centered between materialism and Christianity. People feel those two to be concrete powers that each know what they want. All other worldviews are present in seed form but barely register in the struggle [to capture] minds.

That is the tragedy of modernism. Many noble minds have supported modernism and have given their powers to it. Nonetheless, it seems to have been powerless to take hold of an entire people. The people have actually appropriated only this from modernism: that nothing really matters, that we can do whatever we want, that there is no God to whom we must give an account.[1] It is a sorry fact shown to us with tremendous clarity by history. Viewed at large, the spiritual dichotomy of our days is nothing other than [the dichotomy] of materialism and Christianity.

When someone asks how this came about, a number of assumptions can be put forward. One can say that it is too difficult for ordinary people to approach the refined, subtle assumptions contained within philosophical systems. A profound difference can be made between the "civilized" and the ordinary people, the intellectual and the general population. One can say that the people want concrete slogans, firm guidelines, and have no feeling for the strivings of those of nobler mind. That is correct, I think, only in a very relative sense. If there is a distinction between the "intellectual" and the ordinary people, it would have to consist in this: that the intellectual considers more, looks at life more externally, while the people live more, feel the practice of life more as a reality. That is a difference that undoubtedly exercises much influence. It goes along with this, for example, that the "people" experience philosophical systems as too speculative. [Those systems] have too little firm foundation in the everyday practice of their existence. It offers too little firm foundation against temptation, [too little] an ideal for life, [too little] support in difficulties and worries, [too little] comfort in dying. But what lies behind all that is especially this: insofar as they come into contact with all those philosophical systems, the people feel, naturally, that these [systems] are more or less untrue. I use that word with a certain hesitancy, because it applies to the deepest minds in our history: Spinoza, Kant, and Hegel, and so many other exceptional thinkers.

And what is it that is untrue [about these systems]? It is that they approach God in their thinking, that they climb up toward him, and then that, in actual fact, they deny him. It is that they grasp him with one hand and throw him away with the other. It is that they seek him

---

1   K. H. Roessingh, *Het modernisme in Nederland* (Haarlem: F. Bohn, 1922), 171.

and lift themselves up toward him, and when they approach him, they push him away.

And (I say this again with hesitancy, with honor, even!) untrueness is there. You will always notice it in all those philosophical thoughts. It runs through all these ideas like a fine thread that you see only with difficulty but that you always intuitively suppose to be there.

English empiricism and deism believe in God. They speak about him as the Creator of all things. They approach him in their thinking. And yet they throw him away, into an endless distance. God is so far away, so difficult to reach. And also, he is not empirically perceivable! On earth, we deal with only the visible and sensible. They stretch their hand out to God, and they come close to him; they let that hand fall, and they pull it back. And God recoils into the infinitely distant.

Spinozism (once again, used by me with hesitancy because Spinoza was one of the most religious thinkers ever produced by Europe!) believes in God. It assumes him and speaks about him. But the concept of God that it accepts is so thin, so untouchable, that it cannot be the foundation for religious thought. In contrast to him, there is no sin, because sin is ultimately a moment in him. He is God and the world at the same time. This concept of God flees into something unreal. It is robbed of holiness. Spinozism stretches out its hand toward him, but when it approaches him, it pulls that hand back. God is the substance, the ethereal, the indescribable.

The Kantian system believes in God. It approaches God in explanation of pure, just as much as of practical, reason. But the God whom it knows is not a real power. He is the sanction of our moral consciousness. We postulate him. He does not speak. He does not act. He does not live. He is an idea, a necessary wish. Kant stretches his hand out toward him, but when he approaches him, he pulls that hand back.

Mysticism, finally—and here I mean the sort that makes itself known distinctly from all religion in response to revelation [*openbaringsreligie*]—believes in God. It feels God; it experiences God. But in contrast to us, as those who seek, that God is complete rest. All action lies on our part. God is no living, real power. He neither speaks nor acts. He is reduced to something very delicate, to something very ethereal, but also to something dead. Mysticism stretches out its hand toward him, but when it approaches him, it pulls its hand back.

Now, that is all something that the "people"—the "people" who live, who feel their sin, who experience the mighty power of temptation and also the bitter reality of suffering—regard as untrue. This is why, ultimately, they prefer the brutal denial of God—completely rejecting him—to the nuanced thought that approaches and dethrones him in the same moment. But that is also why they know and feel the real power of the gospel, because the gospel confesses a *living* God. Religion is not a luxury article or an evening mood. If the gospel is anything, it must be a living connection of the living human being to the living God, the God who speaks and who acts!

Now obviously, all this says very little about the truth of the gospel. Someone can agree with this argument without confessing the truthfulness of Christianity. Someone could say, "If faith in a God will ever mean anything to us, the essence of it must be faith in a living God." With this, naturally, the question whether that "living" God exists has not yet been answered. Certainty on this issue must be acquired in another manner. Religious certainty does not rest on arguments for the usefulness of religion. It is something distinct and cannot be closely analyzed. In the final instance, it is born from that unshakable and incomprehensible sense that the human being can be captivated when he stands before Jesus and before his word: "I believe this, and so it is." There is a rapport. The deepest and most intimate connection comes between [Jesus] and the soul, and the soul says yes to him: "You are . . . the Son of the living God!" [Matt. 16:16].

But when this [intuition] is present, a living religion is born. Then the word becomes a power in that person's life. It sheds light on all the events of life; it is made that person's own in ever-increasing richness; it is always new because in its truth it is always shedding light on life itself. Thus, it not only had but continues to have the power not only to bind a few people of aristocratic mind but to rule whole peoples under its leading. Even now, it is the case that when the Eastern person who—from his deep thought on the infinite stillness that transcends him—is brought into contact with the gospel that God is love, compassionate love, he experiences that as the life-renewing [power of] the gospel: faith in the living God.

You must not think that a worldview changes your whole life in a single moment. Life is composed of material that is much too cumbersome to be turned upside down just like that. Far more profound changes are possible in the spheres of abstract thought than in the daily practice of our existence. Someone who recognizes and confesses the Christian world-and-life view as the truth is not yet freed from all his un-Christian behaviors in that moment. Tension always remains between worldview and personality, and while that is true in general, it is particularly true with regard to the gospel.

Conversely, the power of worldview should not be underestimated. Above all, its influence on the passage of generations is incalculable. The life of nations, and of generations, very slowly adapts itself to the worldviews that lie rooted in them. This is true to the extent that often, long after the worldview itself has been rejected, all sorts of powers that sprang from it remain in effect. In Europe in our day, numerous Christian tendencies remain active, even among those who in actual fact are clueless about Christianity itself. You see this most strongly when you enter a world that was formed by other worldviews. The East, for example, is thus so wholly different because very different religions dominated there for centuries. In how people think about marriage, the position of the woman [in society], good and evil, suffering and death, state and government, nature and culture—in short, the East differs from the West on every point. And behind the West's position, there is always something [that has sprung] from Christianity. On every side, Christianity has influenced our culture much more deeply than many would dare to suppose. Long after the faith itself has disappeared, its effects can be seen in every part of human existence.

But this is not to say that this power cannot slowly diminish. Now that the majority of [Western] peoples have become estranged from the gospel of Christ, life has slowly begun to cut its ties with him. Most people feel their existence to be normless and goalless. They do not look at life with the happy smile that comes with a [sense of] vocation. They go [into life] like drifting ships that do not know [*weten*] which course to take. Anyone who takes a closer look at our world will see that. Normlessness in business and industry, in marriage and morality, normlessness produced by the complete lack of a world-and-life view. The West's crisis is that it knows [*kent*] no faith, no worldview, no religion. Its thinkers and seekers labor at this in vain. The only thing that can give a human being a firm foundation and strength is faith in a living God. Every personality needs a worldview to set its norms and limits, to confirm, orient, and support it—[a worldview] that can regulate and shape the powers contained with [that personality] and that can give it direction. Personality and worldview thus belong to one another very closely. As soon as the personality loses that firm foundation, and thus [starts to] live from an intuitively grasped life-vision [*levensvisie*], the personality becomes its own norm, and it loses all orientation to something higher than itself.

All this is able to impress on us the importance of our life. The struggle of worldviews is not a game; we cannot look down on it while shrugging our shoulders. It is extremely serious. Do not say to me, "Whether or not I have a worldview, not much changes in my life." It changes a great deal. If you do not see that in the small things of your life, you will see it in the great things of history. The total lack of worldview disrupts Western life at every level of the population. It leaves people rudderless and without meaning. We must sense our great common task and seek the truth because only the truth can set us free—free from ourselves.

The person who recognizes the gospel, the word, who receives it with that great inner yes, who is full of wonder—that person does not instantly become a perfect person. The word has great power and does a great deal [in his life], but something else must also happen. Or actually, when that person says yes to the word, that change has already happened in principle. That change itself is the new birth, becoming a new person. God does this; it is a speaking of God in the soul that no one else can describe: you hear the sound, and you do not know where it comes from. Only when that has taken place in the deepest part of the human soul does his life become different. Only then can he recognize the word in Jesus, can the human being say yes to him and accept him warmly with his whole heart. Then that word becomes more lively within him. The two lines of worldview and personality bend into each other more and more. The personality is pulled upward by the word, until everything within that person that is at enmity has been broken by the word, and [the word] has captivated him entirely. And so, in all its layers, life has been penetrated by what God has said and done.

Then you see that in the background to all philosophical thought there lies the great paradox that tears our personality apart. All human seeking is a seeking after God, "that they should . . . feel their way toward him and find him" [Acts 17:27]. The pagan does this by naively creating images and believing stories. The Western thinker also does this. All thinking climbs up from the relative to the absolute. However you label it, whether you title it substance or will, the unconscious or reason, whether you describe it as deed or point to it as the infinite, it is always the same. The human being can find no rest in the world of sensations and without noticing it takes a leap toward the eternal. All thinking ends in God, and that all the more strongly if it is deeper and more mature. In this, there lies something that fills us with joy and emotion. Nonetheless, though, thought and life also contain a fleeing from God: approaching him and, when you have come close to him, evading him; climbing up toward him and, when you have made the ascent toward him, shunning him—whether that be by placing him at an endlessly far-off distance, whether that be by making him so vague and ethereal that no relationship with him is possible. This paradox is so universal and so noticeable that it cannot be thought of as an incidental phenomenon. Rather, it must be seen as a clear symptom of the life of the personality.

In that regard, the personality itself is torn and distorted. The human heart thirsts for God, needs God, feels dependent on him, and at the same time stands in enmity against him. It is a not willing and yet also a willing,

a seeking that is no seeking. That contrariety in the human soul finds
its deepest roots in the fact that in his own *I*-ness, the human being
does not want to be ruled by God; that in his *I*-ness, he has grasped
for the ideal of having "equality with God" [Phil. 2:6] and must hold
God outside the sphere of his life with wordless resolve. As soon as
someone places himself in a living and conscious relationship to God,
he is humbled and in sorrow must judge his own life and in humility
must submit himself to him. It is the overcharged feeling of *I* that continually causes a person to reject the same God he seeks. The threefold
impulse in the human soul—toward himself, toward his neighbor, and
toward God—is not harmonious, is not balanced. The desire to be
an individual, the urge for self-maintenance, self-development, self-
rule, overgrows the two other [desires—i.e., for God and neighbor]
and skews the balance within that person. That skewed balance must
emerge in every way he reveals his life, and thus also in his worldview.
The worldview thought of by a human being, born of a human being,
must lay bare the same contortions of the fundamental capacities of
his very existence. That is the deepest cause of this "seeking but not
seeking," this "willing but not willing."

This is why the Christian religion assures us so emphatically, "The
human being can never get there, can never find the truth." Perhaps
he could do so if his thought transcended life, if there was no deeper
connection between personality and worldview. Now, though, no
worldview—however deep and objective—overcomes the worldvision
that slumbers inside a person as an unconscious assumption. Thinking, after all, is at the same time a matter of willing. We are not free
and unprejudiced; we are bound to our own soul, to our own deepest
tendencies. The truth can only be thought of by God and can only
be given to us. The human being cannot create it, cannot produce it.
Rather, he can only receive it. And even when he receives it, he still
feels that this truth is not "according to man," does not correspond
to his own secret will, and that it compels him to the most complete
self-denial. For this reason, he cannot receive it from himself. Rather,
it is the power of God within him that binds the human being to the

truth, that makes him submit to that truth. Thinking is always a moral task. There is a close rapport between thinking and living. Standing in our way on the path toward the truth is sin, the slumber and darkness that descends on our soul through sin. But the same also applies to the truth: it alone can set a person free.

Finally, when we take stock at this point and return to the great questions from which we first set out, we can lay out our results approximately like this:

In the first chapter, we noticed that there is always a twofold connection between personality and worldview. On the one side, every worldview thought up by a human is a revelation of the personality, of who that person is. The worldview is the revelation of the personality. Conversely, each worldview is an attempt at conquering the self, at freeing yourself from your subjective worldvision, and at basing your life on an objective foundation. You can clearly point out these two traits in the history of philosophy. Empiricism, for example, was a grasping [at the truth], a subjective vision, but the history of empiricism shows us that thinking has tried to rise above that grasping. [The reasons for] the downfall of empiricism can be found in its own history. Rationalism was a grasping [at the truth] but a grasping that was corrected in the history of worldview. We find a much deeper foundation in Kant's philosophy, a much more objective foundation. And yet in his system there was also a great deal of that grasping, of his intuitive worldvision, that he never overcame. These two traits run through the entirety of the history of worldview. It is always the personality that reveals itself in the worldview and, at the same time, that tries to conquer itself in the process.

This grasping, however, is especially powerful in the deepest questions, in the questions about God and his relationship to the soul. There the mind's intuition dominates. There thinking loses its objectivity and is moved by the hidden powers of the personality. The more the questions in discussion relate to our life, with the whole posture of our life, the more it becomes impossible to be free of our spontaneous [intuitive] choice. That is why, as we saw, precisely in those highest questions, every worldview so clearly continues to bear the traits of the heart and is a revelation of the tendencies that move that heart. In the worldview, you can see the projection of what is in that human being and thus also the contrariety that holds the human being prisoner.

Must we then end by concluding [that the answer lies in] relativism? Must we then say, "Worldview is a revelation of personality, and so one person cannot convince another, and every person has his own truth. What does it matter to me how another person thinks? I have my own thoughts, my own worldview. A worldview is not an approach to the truth but rather a making plain of the powers that move the personality. And as such, I can live as I want and do not need to be held back by someone else's norms and vision. And as such, everyone has an equal right and cannot rule over anyone else. Every worldview is allowed, and none of them can pretend to have found the truth"? [In that case,] psychology devours philosophy, and relativism means the end of all science. That psychologically motivated relativism is one of the greatest dangers of our modern culture because it busies itself with undermining all stability and destroys life itself. The question will be whether our modern culture ever overcomes this current of thought. If it does not conquer it, this direction will bring about the greatest damage and misery.

Two ideas can be brought into view against this relativism. The first is that a person's worldview is not only a self-revelation but also an overcoming of the self (even if it is often only no more than an attempt at this). In the history of worldviews, there is also an objective moment that always corrects the intuitive worldvision. Thus, in the history of worldviews there is also a certain progress and also development. Questions are better considered in their consequences and are posed from more angles. The long history of human thought has not been without its fruit. Ultimately, this does not prevent the same directions from returning (in new garb). Indeed, in the deepest questions, the worldview can never free itself from the life of the personality because our thinking is always at the same time a matter of our intellect and heart.

Is relativism right when it touches on the deeper questions? Is there progress only in the incidentals—in the ways worldviews are dressed up—but never in their essence? Whether someone counts himself a deist or a pantheist, a theist or an atheist, a pessimist or an optimist, whether someone believes in unshakable moral norms or does not believe in them at all, is that all defined only by personality? Is it the personality that gives the worldview its form? And if that is so, do we then find ourselves again facing the consequences of relativism? Why do we need someone else's worldview? It does not fit our personalities. Indeed, it is not "true" for our personalities.

Against this, only the following can be said: all this would be correct, in a certain sense, if there were only worldviews that were born of human beings—if there were no revelation, or the word thought from God, given by God, that was thus objective, that could and would have to be a guiding standard. If there were only worldviews discovered by people, every person would be able to set himself against the worldviews of other people. If there is revelation, however, as soon as God speaks and breaks human darkness, everything changes. The human being gains a firm place to stand. Certainly, once again, it then comes down to faith, but then that faith, in a certain sense, is a requirement on God's part, in seeking a human being whom he will set free.

For this reason, relativism is indeed a worldview: it makes a choice. It appears to give equal justification to every worldview. In reality, though, it makes a choice. It is justified only if there is no God, or at least no living God, when there is no "word" given by God. The premise of relativism is the idea that every worldview is born of personality and reflects who that person is. This premise is permissible only when the person first admits that there is no revelation, no word. But then, latently as it may be, perhaps unconsciously, he has already determined his posture. He has already cut off one path. The only one that he can ever find is faith in a dead God, in complete silence.

Belief in revelation cuts through relativism. It breaks relativism. It brings calm in the midst of the commotion caused by worldviews. We can retain that belief only when we remember clearly that the gospel was not a human product, that it cannot be born of the human being, because it breaks the human being inwardly, because it does not know the dichotomy of the heart that seeks God without seeking and that finds God without finding him. The gospel portrays a living posture toward the living God. That is something that a human being always sidesteps—and must sidestep—because while there is a mysterious compulsion within his essence that is drawn toward God, he also never wants to follow it.

Looking on philosophy from the vantage point of psychology is a beautiful task. It clarifies our insight into the building of systems. It makes us see that behind worldviews there are human hearts that grapple with one another. It makes comprehensible the passion with which the struggle between worldviews is often carried out. It makes us understand why the possession of a worldview is indispensable for a human being.

You could say, "Tell me who you are, and I will tell you what your world-view will be like." You could also invert this: "Tell me what your worldview is like, and I will tell what you will become." A worldview is able to build up a person's life but is also powerful enough to leave it in ruins. A worldview can pull a life apart, can tear up a human being and leave all norms in tatters. That may not always be evident in the small things of someone's life, but it will certainly be proved with tremendous clarity in the course of history. Worldviews last for longer than one generation. One generation can celebrate worldviews that provide no foundation for its own life and without that generation's exterior taking on noticeable damage. This is so because for all of us, our hearts are unconsciously so Christian. But subsequent generations will reveal that revolution more strongly because the foundation has been lost.

The emergency facing our Western world is its lack of a worldview. It has no life-nourishing and life-directing idea and therefore also no unity in living and thinking. On the basis of all that has been said, I may now say more strongly: the emergency facing our Western world is its loss of Christianity—the lack of true religion, of self-denial, of sacrifice, of faith, of trust, of a sense of shame, of hope in God. Our

[Western] world could fall apart through that emergency. Our society will become disjointed and desolate when it is not borne up by great ideals, by life-preserving norms.

The royal word of Jesus Christ stands opposite that emergency:

Everyone who practices sin is a slave to sin. . . . If the Son sets you free, you will be free indeed. [John 8:34, 36]

You will know the truth, and the truth will set you free. [John 8:32]

General Index

Abraham, 153
absentmindedness, 49
activity, 98, 114, 115
agency, 18
Ahura Mazda, 61
Alexandrian Neoplatonism, 69
ambition, 51
American evangelicalism, 4–8, 18
Angra Mainyu, 62
animism, 60
Anschauungsformen, 127, 130
anthroposophy, 144
antithesis, 122
appearances, 136
aprioristic forms, 11, 57, 127, 128, 130,
    132–33, 135, 137
architecture, 80–82
Aristotle, 84, 85, 88n11, 101, 102, 105,
    143
art, 71, 80, 81, 125, 144
asceticism, 71, 148
assumptions, 15, 25
as though, 34, 35, 37
astronomy, 88
atheism, 33, 74
atheistic materialism, 166
atman, 64–67, 163
attributes, 92–93, 108, 112, 113
Aufgabe, 55, 56
Augustine, 16–17
authority, 101, 102, 126, 136
autonomy, 159
Avesta, 61

Bacon, Francis, 84–87
Bavinck, Coenraad Bernardus, 9
Bavinck, Herman, 6, 7, 8, 10, 13
Bavinck, J. H., 8–22
Bavinck, Maarten, 21
beauty, 58, 113, 125
being, and thinking, 30, 107, 117
"biblical worldview," x, 2, 7
bird's-eye view, 12
Brahma, 64, 163
British culture, 3–5
Brock, Cory, xi, 7
Buddhism, 2, 20, 143
Burckhardt, Jacob, 20n19
Byron, George Gordon, 124

Calvin, John, 3, 5
Cambridge University, 91
Çankara, 66
Cartesius, 106, 107, 109, 110, 111. *See
    also* Descartes, René
cartography, 8, 14
categories, 129, 130, 132, 137–38
causality, 86, 87–89, 94, 95, 129, 134,
    140, 159
certainty, 104, 109, 119
Chandogya Upanishad, 65n8
Christianity
    and mysticism, 70, 147, 157
    and personality, 77
    and truth, 37
    and Western culture, 19
Christian Science, 144

Scripture Index